19:7x

Any Questions about these poetry
please Contact your nearest
Shia Imami Ismaili Centre" only

Only copy in
SWAN

Thanks

JAN   1998

SHIMMERING LIGHT

Shimmering
LIGHT

An Anthology of Ismaili Poetry

Translated into English by
FAQUIR MUHAMMAD HUNZAI

Introduced and Edited by
KUTUB KASSAM

I. B. Tauris Publishers
LONDON · NEW YORK

in association with

The Institute of Ismaili Studies
LONDON

Published in 1996 by
I.B.Tauris & Co Ltd
45 Bloomsbury Square
London WC1A 2HY
175 Fifth Avenue
New York NY 10010

In the United States of America
and in Canada distributed by
St Martin's Press
175 Fifth Avenue
New York NY 10010

A full CIP record for this book is available from the
British Library

A full CIP record for this book is available from the
Library of Congress

Library of Congress catalog card number: available

ISBN 1 85043 907 9

Typeset in Monotype Ehrhardt
by Lucy Morton, London SE12

Printed and bound in Great Britain
by WBC Ltd, Bridgend, Mid-Glamorgan

Contents

THE INSTITUTE OF ISMAILI STUDIES, LONDON

The Institute of Ismaili Studies was established in 1977 with the object of promoting scholarship and learning on Islam, in the historical as well as contemporary context, and a better understanding of its relationship with other societies and faiths.

The Institute's programmes encourage a perspective which is not confined to the theological and religious heritage of Islam, but seeks to explore the relationship of religious ideas to broader dimensions of society and culture. They thus encourage an inter-disciplinary approach to the materials of Islamic history and thought. Particular attention is also given to issues of modernity that arise as Muslims seek to relate their heritage to the contemporary situation.

Within the Islamic tradition, the Institute's programmes seek to promote research on those areas which have had relatively lesser attention devoted to them in secondary scholarship to date. These include the intellectual and literary expressions of Shi'ism in general, and Ismailism in particular.

In the context of Islamic societies, the Institute's programmes are informed by the full range and diversity of cultures in which Islam is practised today, from the Middle East, Southern and Central Asia and Africa to the industrialized societies of the West, thus taking into consideration the variety of contexts which shape the ideals, beliefs and practices of the faith.

The publications of the Institute fall into several distinct categories:

1   Occasional papers or essays addressing broad themes of the relationship between religion and society in the historical as well as modern context, with special reference to Islam, but encompassing, where appropriate, other faiths and cultures.

2   Proceedings of conferences or symposia.

3   Works exploring a specific theme or aspect of Islamic faith or culture, or the contribution of an individual figure or writer.

4   Translations of poetic or literary texts.

5   Editions or traslations of significant texts of a primary or secondary nature.

6   Ismaili Studies.

In facilitating these and other publications, the Institute's sole aim is to encourage original, interesting and mature thought, scholarship and analysis of the relevant issues. There will naturally be a diversity of views, ideas and interpretations, and the opinions expressed will be those of the authors.

This book falls into category 4 listed above.

Acknowledgements

A work of this scope and nature could not be completed without the generosity of spirit and the practical and timely aid of many people. This work is therefore dedicated to those without whose help it would have been impossible to complete it. First, I would like to thank Dr. Aziz Esmail for the initial suggestion of this work, and Dr. Farhad Daftary for his encouragement and making available to me his research on Alamut and post-Alamut Ismaili poets. I am grateful for the editorial and creative input of Kutub Kassam who undertook the difficult task of rendering the translations into verse. My sincere thanks are also due to Dr. Jalal Badakhchani and Alnoor Merchant for their assistance. My wife, Rashida Noormohamed-Hunzai, who despite her own demanding schedule has devoted countless hours to type, edit and correct the manuscript, deserves special thanks. I would also like to express my gratitude to the following friends and colleagues: Zahir Lalani for his crucial technical assistance which has been well beyond the call of friendship, Sadruddin Fattoum for his constructive suggestions in the translations of some of the Arabic *qasa'id*, and Ghulam Abbas Hunzai for his constant support.

FMH

Foreword

The literatures of the Islamic peoples are rarely known to Western
readers, except for a few classics such as the poetry of Hafiz, the
mystical verses of Mawlana Rumi and, in the Anglo-Saxon world,
Omar Khayyam's *Ruba'iyyat*. The paucity of reliable translations and
of introductions into the complicated web of rhetorical devices, of
allusions to the Qur'an and the Prophetic tradition, the rich colours
of hyperbolic speech and the measureless feelings expressed by the
poets make it difficult for a non-tutored reader to appreciate this
poetry in all its dazzling beauty. And even less known than Islamic
poetry in general is that of the Ismaili community, for the literature
of this community was kept as a secret, not available to the outsider.
Yet, a single glance at Ismail Poonawala's bibliography of Ismaili
literature makes the curious reader aware of the enormous number of
important sources, and the scholar is happy to see that these spiritual
treasures are being unveiled before the eyes of scholars.

Among those who are connected with Ismaili literature one name,
however, was known for a long time: that of Nasir-i Khusraw (d. after
1072 in northern Badakhshan). His travelogue, *Safarnama*, was
formerly often used in European universities as the first reading book
in Persian for its deceptively easy style. The *Safarnama* was edited
and translated into French first by Ch. Schefer of Paris in 1881;
during the same decade the German scholar H. Ethé as well as the
French orientalist E. Fagnan edited and analysed some other works of
the great philosopher-poet. E.G. Browne, well-known for his
pioneering work on Persian literature, considered Nasir-i Khusraw
one of the very rare Persian poets whose work would appeal to
Western readers as he does not indulge in panegyric poetry but speaks

honestly out of his heart, defending the true faith and scolding those who misunderstand and misinterpret the message of the Qu'ran, the words of the Prophet and of his heirs, the children of Fatima. However, despite E.G. Browne's enthusiastic praise of Nasir-i Khusraw's poetry, which was published in 1905, very few attempts were made to offer his verse, at least in part, to an anglophone audience, and only in 1992 the present writer's book *Make a Shield from Wisdom* appeared under the auspices of the Institute of Ismaili Studies. As for the major philosophical work of this great thinker, *Jami' al-Hikmatayn*, it was edited and analysed by Henry Corbin in 1953, and translated into French by Isabelle de Gastines in 1990.

Yet, for the mainstream orientalist, Nasir-i Khusraw's poetry remained outside the normal course of Islamic studies, and only recently deeper research into his fascinating thought has begun. But who would have imagined that translations from his *Diwan* would be included in a collection of Ismaili devotional poetry?

One may compare his verse to the work of Ibn Hani, who lived a century before him in the farthest west of the Islamic world, in Andalusia, where he used his highly hyperbolical language to emphasize the Ismaili *da'wa*, the call to the "true religion" – so much so that he had to leave his native country to become the panegyrist of al-Mu'izz, the Fatimid caliph who after the conquest of Egypt in 969 AD founded Cairo, *al-Qahira al-Mu'izziyya*, the capital of the Fatimid empire in which, under the inspiring rule of the Imam of the time, happiness and wealth seemed to reign and people prosper, as Nasir-i Khusraw shows in both his *Safarnama* and in some of his auto-biographical poems.

Arabic and Persian poetry in honour of the true Imam and of the Ismaili faith were by no means restricted to the classical time when the "Fatimid Sun", as Nasir-i Khusraw sometimes calls it, was shining over parts of the East. Pious poets have poured out their hearts wherever small pockets of Ismailis were found, be it in Syria, be it in Eastern Iran, in Badakhshan, where Nasir-i Khusraw is still venerated as a miraculous saint and wise philosopher, and somewhat later in the vast areas of the western subcontinent, from Gujarat to the Panjab. There, the devotional songs of the community, the *ginan*s, were composed, again, in a large variety of languages – songs, in which the Indian traditional imagery is used side by side with the philosophical vocabulary of the Ismaili tradition. These *ginan*s again deserve an in-depth study owing to their linguistic problems and the complicated Khojki alphabet in which they were noted down till recently – it is to be hoped that an anthology similar to the present one will be published before long to highlight the deep feelings of the community for their spiritual leader. And if the different yet familiar idioms of India and Pakistan were not enough to make our access to Ismaili devotional literature difficult, what can be said of hymns in Burushaski, a language absolutely unrelated to any other known language, and spoken to this day in the high valleys of Hunza?

It is not only the fact that most of the classical Ismaili writings were hidden for centuries that has made this literature difficult to appreciate; the different languages used by the Ismaili community during the past millennium have meant that this literature has been a closed book for most people, even within the community – for a Syrian or Iranian Ismaili was or is not able to read and enjoy religious poetry in Sindhi, Burushaski or Shina, while the pious in the lowlands of Sind or Cutch might not be conversant with Arabic or Persian.

For this reason a collection of Ismaili religious poetry in translation is most welcome to both the insider and the outsider. In this volume we follow the translators through their fine English renderings of a number of selected pieces from many of the linguistic areas in which Ismaili communities lived and still live, and we read with joy and deep admiration the poets' various statements about the true faith, about the radiance of the Imam whose *didar* is the hoped-for goal of the believer. The strong faith which has inspired the original pieces is certainly reflected in the translators' work, and every reader, from whatever religious background he or she may come, will, I am convinced, enjoy this anthology and experience the intensity of religious feeling that touches his or her own heart.

The poems show a beautiful way to the "shimmering light" the poets have seen in their visions, a way that will inspire their readers.

We hope, therefore, that the anthology may serve as a fine introduction into a hitherto closed and mysterious world, a world filled with ardent spiritual love and inexhaustible beauty.

Annemarie Schimmel
Bonn, Spring 1995

Introduction

One of the most remarkable transformations in Islamic studies during the twentieth century has been in the understanding of Ismailism. As a result of the pioneering work of many scholars, especially since the 1930s, there has been rapid progress in the study of Ismaili history and thought, and a fundamental re-evaluation of the Ismaili contributions to the intellectual and cultural development of Islam. But in spite of this decisive achievement, there are many aspects of Ismailism which remain obscure or have received insufficient attention in scholarly enquiry. One such area concerns the poetic tradition of the Ismailis, the investigation of which has been on the whole limited and fragmentary. This gap is surprising in view of the large corpus of Ismaili poetic literature which exists, and the fact that some of the foremost Ismaili thinkers were adept at writing in both prose and poetry.[1]

To be sure, a promising start has been made in recent decades with the publication of critical editions of some Ismaili poetic works and specialized studies on the devotional poetry of Ismailis in the Indian subcontinent. But with the exception of a few poets such as Nasir-i Khusraw, whose works have been partially translated, much of this literature remains inaccessible to those unfamiliar with the original languages in which it was composed. It is to address this situation that the reader is offered here for the first time a compilation of Ismaili poems and verses from Arabic and Persian in English translation. This anthology is intended, among other things, to demonstrate the poetic achievements of the Ismailis in Egypt, Syria, Iran and Central Asia over a period of more than a thousand years.

The majority of the poems in this volume are religious and

I

devotional in character, although it should be noted that the Ismaili poetic tradition is not concerned exclusively with the expression of religious and moral sentiments. The predominance of the spiritual element, however, requires that any examination of Ismaili poetry be situated within the general context of religious poetry in Islam, for it is only in relation to the larger tradition that it can be properly assessed.

The earliest examples of religious poetry in Islam are to be found in the verses of a small group of poets who were contemporaries of the Prophet Muhammad. The most reputed of these was Hassan ibn Thabit (d. c. 50/669) whose poems in praise of the Prophet and his companions performed an important role in counteracting the hostile verses of the Qurayshi poets who were opposed to him. Hassan's poetry was motivated by a personal reverence for the Prophet, but it was also intended to champion the new social and religious order inaugurated by the Prophet and to denigrate the cause of his enemies and detractors, as was customary in the poetic discourse of pre-Islamic Arabia. In the years following the Prophet's death in 11/632, a number of his companions and their associates are also known to have composed eulogies in his memory or occasional verses inspired by passages of the Qur'an.[2]

With the rise of the Umayyad dynasty in 41/661, a kind of religio-political verse emerged among various social and religious groups who were disaffected by the new regime. The poetry of the Kharijis, which has survived only in a fragmentary form, is notable for its militant rhetoric and passion for martyrdom. A less combative and more devotional note is found in the poetical writings of the early Shi'i groupings, such as the Kaysanis and the Zaydis. Among their leading poets were Kuthayyir 'Azza (d. 105/723–4) and al-Sayyid al-Himyari (d. 171/787–8). But the most talented was al-Kumayt ibn Zayd al-Asadi (d. 126/743), who was imprisoned by the Umayyads and later murdered in mysterious circumstances. The poems of al-Kumayt are highly regarded by the Shi'is, in particular his lengthy composition, *al-Hashimiyyat*, which is among the earliest literary records of a distinctive Muslim piety focused upon devotion to the *ahl al-bayt*, the Prophet and his family.[3]

One of the interesting features of Arabic poetry in the first two centuries of Islam is that it was largely non-religious in outlook. Although most of the poets who flourished under the Umayyad and early 'Abbasid dynasties made occasional use of Islamic imagery and religious ideas in their verses, they were largely preoccupied by the themes typified in the main genres of classical Arabic poetry such as the panegyric or praise-poem (*madih*), love lyrics (*ghazal*), hunting poems (*tardiyyat*), wine songs (*khamriyyat*), polemics (*naqa'id*) and satire (*hija'*). In fact, religious or ascetical verses as such (*zuhdiyyat*) constituted a small portion of the enormous output of poetry in this period, and Arabic literary theory of the time does not seem to have recognized the religious element as a distinctive poetic motif.

The development of a substantive tradition of religious poetry in Islam is associated with the emergence in the second half of the second/eighth century of a complex, widespread movement for moral and religious reform. It arose partly in reaction to what was generally perceived as the worldly character of the Umayyad ruling class, but essentially it was the outcome of the increasing integration of Islam in social life. This process intensified after the 'Abbasid revolution of 132/750, when different theological and legal schools began to be formulated and the various communities of Islam started to acquire their identities. Another important feature of the religious and cultural transformation of Muslim society during this period was the growing interest in the spiritual and mystical life of Islam which later came to be known as *tasawwuf* or Sufism. It is from the second century of the Islamic era that we have some of the early evidence of individuals seeking a more personal and interiorized experience of faith, and it was out of this engagement that there appeared amongst them a highly introspective, intensely personal kind of religious poetry.[4]

The new religious poetry was at first deeply austere and puritanical, reflecting the ascetical, self-denying lives of the poets. Their consciousness was dominated by the fear of God and renunciation of the world, as in the writings of Abu'l-Atahiya (d. 210/826), who is regarded as the first religious poet of genius in Islam. The same disposition is also found in the epigrammatic verses of Rabi'a al-'Adawiyya (d. 185/801), the famous woman mystic of Basra, although it was

3

tempered by a spirit of devotional love. In the next century, however, the fear of God and His wrath in the hereafter gave way to the personal love of Him and a quest for divine union in this world. The finest expressions of this development are found in the mystical love-poems of Dhu'l-Nun the Egyptian (d. 246/861), and the enigmatic verses of Mansur al-Hallaj, who was crucified in Baghdad in 309/922 on spurious charges of having claimed, among other things, divinity for himself.

In the last years of his imprisonment, al-Hallaj composed his famous prose-poem, the *Kitab al-tawasin*, which contains a eulogic description of the Prophet Muhammad as the pre-eternal light of prophecy issuing from the divine effulgence.[5] This is considered to be the first reference in Sufi literature to a motif that was already well-established in early Shi'i tradition and poetic literature of the first century. It provided a fresh impetus to the development of the *na'tiyya*, poems in honour and praise of the Prophet, which later became perhaps the most popular genre of religious poetry in all the languages and cultures of Islam. It was partly through this medium that the veneration of the Prophet became an essential part of Muslim piety and a strong uniting force among Muslims to this day.[6]

In the two centuries after the death of Mansur al-Hallaj, there appears to have been a certain sparsity in the creation of exceptional mystical verse, although Sufism as a way of life began to spread widely in the Muslim world and some of the classical works of theoretical Sufism were produced in this period. It was not until the sixth/twelfth century that the Sufi poets, reinvigorated by new ideas and fresh creative impulses, began to compose some of the most original and outstanding mystical poetry in Islamic literature. This achievement is best depicted in the works of Ibn al-Farid (d. 632/1235) and Ibn 'Arabi (d. 638/1240) writing in Arabic, as well as the Persian poetry of Farid al-Din 'Attar (d. c. 622/1225) and Jalal al-Din Rumi (d. 672/1273), the latter acknowledged as the world's greatest mystical poet.

Unlike the earlier period, the Sufi prose and poetry of the new phase has a pronounced theosophical and metaphysical outlook. While the quest for divine love and union continues to dominate everything else, there is an intensification in the veneration of the Prophet Muhammad, who acquires a special ontological status as the perfect man, associated with the divine word and the primordial light of the universe. The major works of Sufi literature from this time also exhibit a profound resonance with Shi'i esoteric and spiritual ideas. The relationship between Shi'ism and Sufism is one of the larger issues of Islamic cultural history which has yet to be investigated fully. Although a number of specialized studies have examined the seminal role of the early Shi'i Imams, especially Ja'far al-Sadiq (d. 148/765), in the formative period of Sufism, we know very little of the precise modes of interface and transmission between them.[7]

The close association of Shi'ism and Sufism was undoubtedly encouraged by the momentous political and cultural changes of the fourth and fifth centuries, when the 'Abbasid empire became fragmented into autonomous or independent states and a reconfigurated, multi-cultural social order emerged in the Muslim world. The Shi'is gained political ascendancy in North Africa, Egypt and Syria under the Fatimid Ismailis, and in Iran and Iraq under the pro-Shi'i Buwayhid dynasty. These circumstances led to a renaissance of Shi'i learning and literature in Arabic and Persian, the intellectual and cultural significance of which is often not recognized in modern scholarship. The poetic expression of the Shi'i devotional spirit acquired its classical form in the works of the Ismaili poets Ibn Hani (d. 362/973) and Nasir-i Khusraw (d. after 465/1072), and the eminent Twelver Shi'i poet and scholar, al-Sharif al-Radi (d. 406/1015). There also appeared a new genre of religious poetry among the Shi'is, the intensely mournful *marthiya* or elegy, to commemorate the martyrdom of the Prophet's grandson, Imam Husayn, at Karbala in 61/680.

The most organized and energetic of the Shi'i communities in the third and fourth centuries were the Ismailis who, as reported by historians and heresiographers of the time, commanded popular support in many parts of the Muslim world. The Ismailis offered a dynamic and progressive vision of social reform, with a sophisticated system of religious and philosophical thought based upon an esoteric understanding of the inner meaning of the Qur'an. The vigorous expansion of Ismailism was largely due to the *da'is*, the missionaries of the Ismaili *da'wa* organization. Although not much is known about its earliest history, the *da'wa* was centrally directed from Syria in the middle of the third/ninth century and thereafter spread rapidly in Iraq, eastern Arabia, Iran, Transoxania, Yemen and North Africa. By 297/909, the Ismailis had successfully established the nucleus of a Fatimid state in Ifriqiya, which was subsequently extended to the whole of North Africa, Sicily, Egypt and the Hijaz.

In the meagre volume of Ismaili literature that has survived from the early period before the Fatimids transferred their headquarters to Egypt there is very little poetic writing. An example of the few pieces that have remained is a series of poems by the *da'i* Ja'far ibn Mansur al-Yaman celebrating Fatimid victories in North Africa in 335/947. There is also a long philosophical *qasida* composed by Abu'l-Haytham al-Jurjani in the first half of the same century, which is among the earliest examples of religious verse in Persian literature. The fact that this poem consists of a series of questions on doctrinal issues, which a century later inspired Nasir-i Khusraw to write one of his major philosophical treatises, indicates that poetry was an important medium of intellectual discourse among the early Ismailis.[8]

From the beginning of their rule and in particular after the occupation of Egypt in 358/969, the Fatimid Imam-caliphs concerned themselves with social reform, the promotion of the arts and the sciences, the construction of mosques, colleges and libraries, and other public projects. The centerpiece of this programme was the foundation of Cairo which became the new capital city of the Fatimids, and the establishment of al-Azhar as its principal mosque and educational complex. The Fatimid encouragement of intellectual and cultural expression attracted numerous scholars, writers, poets and artists to Egypt. Indeed, at the height of its power and prosperity, Fatimid Cairo rivalled 'Abbasid Baghdad as much in the vitality of its cultural life as for political supremacy in the world of Islam.

Among the arts, the cultivation of poetry was especially encouraged by the Imams, several of whom are known to have composed their own poems. As was customary with most ruling Muslim dynasties, the Fatimids maintained a retinue of professional poets, ranked which followed the collapse of the Fatimid state in 567/1171. But there survives the collection of another poet who was a contemporary of Ibn Hani, namely Amir Tamim al-Fatimi (d. 374/984), the eldest son of Imam al-Mu'izz and brother of his successor, Imam al-'Aziz. The poet-prince was a highly accomplished composer of romantic as well as religious verses, which are notable for the way they combine a celebration of human life, love and nature, with deep loyalty and affection for the Imams.

The religious ethos underlying Fatimid court poetry was intimately linked to the spiritual status of the Imam-caliphs and the devotional attitude of the poets towards them. In keeping with their general policy of intellectual and religious tolerance, the Fatimids saw no reason to dictate literary taste to the population at large, but it seems that the poetry which flourished under their rule had a more pronounced devotional spirit the nearer it approached the domain of the court. This aspect is less conspicuous in those poets who were only peripherally attached to the court, such as Abu Raqa'maq (d. 399/1008) who wrote panegyrics for his patron, Ya'qub ibn Killis, the famous *wazir* of Imam al-'Aziz, and Zafir al-Haddad (d. 529/1135), the blacksmith-poet whose verses were much admired by the governor of Alexandria. There were also other poets popular in the streets of Cairo and Damascus who were concerned mainly with non-religious themes of the kind commonplace elsewhere in the Muslim world.[9]

The most significant development in Fatimid poetry after Ibn Hani came not from the environs of the court or the bazaars of Cairo but from the ranks of the Ismaili *da'wa*. In the Fatimid state, the *da'wa* constituted a centralized religious organization parallel to the administrative and military hierarchies of government. Only men of outstanding personality, intelligence and loyalty to the Imam would become *da'is*, usually after intensive training in the Islamic sciences and Ismaili thought. The fact that virtually all the major thinkers, writers and poets in Ismaili literature were associated with the *da'wa* is a measure of the immense intellectual strength and creativity of this institution.

We know very little about the programme for training of the *da'is* in the higher institutions of learning established by the Fatimids, such as al-Azhar and the Dar al-'Ilm. But since a mastery of Arabic language and philology was an essential requirement for the *da'i*s, it is likely that poetics too featured in their studies. There is some evidence that the *da'wa* regarded the poetic medium as an important means of religious and moral education. This is indicated by the existence in Fatimid literature of a number of popular versified treatises called *urjuza* on the basic tenets of the Ismaili faith. Indeed, the most prominent judge and jurist who served under four Fatimid caliphs, al-Qadi al-Nu'man (d. 363/974) himself produced a book on the principles of Ismaili jurisprudence in verse.

But this is not to say that the *da'i*s who composed poetry were primarily concerned with instruction or that their main purpose, as some scholars have presumed, was to spread Fatimid political and religious propaganda. These poets were not really concerned with the expression of a systematic, doctrinally modulated account of Ismaili religious and political thought. Unlike Fatimid scholastic literature which usually conformed to well-defined norms of doctrinal acceptability, the poetry was essentially shaped by the personal feelings and responses of the poets, above all by their devotion to the Imams. It was rooted in and grew out of their encounter with questions of life, faith and destiny, and their quest for spiritual enlightenment.

This point is illustrated by no less a figure than al-Mu'ayyad fi'l-Din al-Shirazi (d. 470/1078), the distinguished chief *da'i* of Imam al-Mustansir, whose writings include a *Diwan* of religious poems. Like Ibn Hani, he too had escaped persecution in his native Persia to serve the Fatimids in Egypt. Al-Mu'ayyad is more renowned in Ismaili studies for his theological lectures and diplomatic skills than for the poetry he composed, which is probably because it has not yet been studied seriously. Al-Mu'ayyad's poems are significant for the thoroughgoing religiosity by which he sets them apart from the political and ceremonial poetry of the court, as well as from the hedonistic inclinations of the plebeian poets. The deeply personal and devotional character of much of his poetry is evident in verses such as these:

Alas, my intellect
has become overcome
and oppressed by
the evil of desire.

Woe to me because
I have wronged myself;
I am beyond neither
blame nor reproach.

O why did I waste
my life when the path
of guidance was open
and spacious to me?

And why did I lose
the light by which
I am related to
the close and noble ones?

Another outstanding Ismaili poet, one who became a close friend of al-Mu'ayyad, was his fellow countryman Nasir-i Khusraw (d. after 465/1072) who visited Cairo for a few years, but spent most of his adult life as a senior Ismaili *da'i* in a remote part of Badakhshan in Central Asia. Here, he wrote his major philosophical works as well as the poems for which he is equally celebrated. Nasir is considered one of the pioneers of Persian prose and poetry, and his writings have had a profound and lasting influence to this day on the Ismaili communities of Iran, Afghanistan, Tajikistan and northern Pakistan.

It is in the *Diwan* of Nasir-i Khusraw that we find perhaps the quintessential expression of Ismaili religious sensibility in poetic form. It is at once contemplative and moralistic, spiritual and philosophical, esoteric and rationalistic, ascetical and mystical. There is also a certain melancholia and world-weariness in his poems, probably arising from his bitter experience of religious persecution over many years. In this attitude as expressed in the following lines, Nasir's work is reminiscent of the critical discontent of the blind poet-philosopher Abu'l-'Ala al-Ma'arri (d. 449/1057), with whom Nasir became acquainted while on his way to Egypt and who later engaged in a vigorous correspondence with al-Mu'ayyad fi'l-Din al-Shirazi on the subject of vegetarianism.[10]

> O do not make business with this world
> which takes from you a cloak for a needle!
>
> I sought its company but found no profit
> from it because it wore me down.
>
> If you cannot escape its friendship,
> how can you be liberated from yourself?
>
> Woe to the one who is imprisoned by himself!
> May he be bankrupt in both the worlds!
>
> This world is the internment of hearts:
> throw away the trapdoor from your hearts!
>
> Your abode is not here but in another
> world which is brilliant and everlasting.

The Fatimid state entered a period of terminal decline in the fifth/
eleventh century as a result of recurrent economic crises, increasing
military interventions in the political and religious affairs of the state,
and a major schism among the Ismailis over succession to the Imamate
which led to the division of the community between the Must'alis and
the Nizaris. At the same time, the eastern Ismailis of Iran and Syria
were coming under severe persecution from the Seljuqs, who had
taken effective control of the 'Abbasid state. It was in these circum-
stances that towards the end of the century the Persian Ismailis, who
were then under the leadership of the *da'i* Hasan-i Sabbah (d. 518/
1124), acquired the fortress of Alamut and a number of other moun-
tainous strongholds in Iran and later Syria, which came to constitute
the territories of an Ismaili state. The long military struggle that en-
sued for almost a century between the Ismailis and the Seljuqs was one
of the most turbulent periods in Ismaili history and later became a
focus of fabulous stories and legends in medieval European literature.[11]
     It is typical of the intellectual concern of the Persian Ismailis that
in spite of the difficult and precarious circumstances of their lives,
they maintained libraries at Alamut and other fortresses, encouraged
scholarly and literary activity, and provided refuge to many non-Ismaili
Muslim and non-Muslim thinkers fleeing from the Mongol invasions
of Central Asia. However, almost all the literature of this period was
lost when the Mongols overwhelmed the Ismaili fortresses of Iran in

654/1256 and set their libraries ablaze. The writings which have survived from the Alamut period include some verses such as the following lines by Ra'is Hasan, which provide a fleeting and poignant testimony to the extraordinary times in which the Ismailis lived, their experiences of hope and despair, their reflections on individual acts of heroism and collective tragedy, and the inspiration of the faith which sustained them:

> O brothers! When the blessed time
> comes and the good fortune of
> both the worlds accompanies us,
> the king who possesses more than
> a hundred thousand horsemen will
> be frightened of a single warrior.
> But it is also possible that when
> our good fortune is on the wane,
> our spring will turn into autumn
> and the autumn into – spring!

In the aftermath of the Mongol invasions, many of the Ismailis who survived the widespread persecution which followed the destruction of their fortresses were obliged to flee Iran or to conceal their identities by associating themselves with diverse Sufi groups. Hence, it is not surprising that there is almost a complete dearth of Ismaili literature in Persian for almost 200 years. The only substantial work by an Ismaili from this bleak period is the poetry of Nizari Quhistani (d. 720/1320). As an educated and ambitious man, it seems that Nizari was able to adapt himself quite successfully to the new social order, since he worked for many years in a local Sunni court as a professional poet and administrator. His poetical works, consisting in the main of a *Diwan* and several long *Mathnawi*s, have barely received any scholarly attention except in Russia. Leaving aside the panegyrics he composed for the local rulers, Nizari's poetry is notable for its expression of Ismaili religious sentiment in the mystical vocabulary of the Sufis. It is sometimes compared to the verses of the great lyrical poet of Persia, Hafiz (d. c. 792/1390), because of the metaphorical ambiguity of its love and wine symbolism.

Nizari's writings are the earliest literary example of what Ivanow called the "coalescence" of Persian Ismailism and Sufism that commenced after the Mongol invasions. In this period of over 600 years, the Persian-speaking Ismaili writers of Iran, Afghanistan and Central Asia resorted to forms of expression which were more closely associated with the Sufis. If Nizari was the first Ismaili writer to make extensive use of Sufi terminology, his case anticipated the even more intensive convergence between Sufism and Shi'ism in Persian culture that occurred in the following centuries. This relationship is reflected not only in the writings of Ismaili authors but also in the poetic and philosophical literature of Twelver Shi'ism. The interface of Shi'ism and Sufism was an elaborate and complex process, of which no detailed study has been undertaken to date. Indeed, so all-pervasive and mutually enriching was this association that, as noted by both Ivanow and Corbin, it is sometimes impossible to tell whether a particular text is of Sufi or Ismaili origin. This is the case, for example, with one of the most popular versified manuals of Persian Sufism, the *Gulshan-i raz* (*Rose-garden of Mystery*) by Mahmud-i Shabistari, a contemporary of Nizari Quhistani whose work incorporates many Ismaili ideas.[12]

Since Ivanow's early researches in Persian Ismailism, it has been taken for granted that the Ismaili writers resorted to Sufism as a means of camouflaging their doctrines in accordance with the age-old Shi'i principle of *taqiyya* or dissimulation of faith. However, this argument fails to discriminate *taqiyya* as a precautionary measure for survival from its function in preserving the *haqa'iq* or esoteric teachings of the Ismailis from those who were unprepared for, or likely to misunderstand, this knowledge. As a general rule, the Ismailis, in common with most Sufi *tariqas*, eschewed the recording of their doctrines in the exoteric sense and revealed the esoteric to only those who had reached the appropriate level of understanding. It is in this sense of *taqiyya* as esoteric prudence that the following lines by Nizari Quhistani are to be understood:

> O Nizari! You have forgotten the secret of
> the "deaf and dumb",
> otherwise you would not read such discourses
> to one born blind.
> How is it possible to open an oyster before
> the blind,

as if you are offering saffron with hay to
a herd of cows?

It is indeed the case that often in times of political persecution the
Ismailis were obliged to conceal their identities, but there is no
evidence that their application of *taqiyya* in the literary domain ever
involved the deliberate interpolation of texts with an extraneous
vocabulary. Thus, Nizari Quhistani's compositions in the Sufi style
can be explained in terms of the deep and lasting transformation of
poetic language in Persian that took place after the Mongol invasions.
This premise is supported by the fact that when Shi'ism later became
the state religion of Iran and the Ismailis were able to reassert their
identity more openly, they continued to retain the mystical lexicon of
Sufism in their literature.

In a more substantive sense, the Shi'i–Sufi association can be under-
stood in terms of the fundamental unity and continuum of esoteric
Islam. The esoteric tradition entered Islamic intellectual thought and
spiritual life from a very early period through a variety of sources and
subsequently emerged in the form of an ecumenical mysticism
acceptable to a majority of Muslims, both Sunni and Shi'i. The close
inter-relationship between the Ismailis and the Sufis may therefore be
viewed as a re-convergence of springs arising from the same spiritual
fountainhead. Doubtless that is why the works of some of the out-
standing poets of Persian Sufism, such as Sana'i, 'Attar and Rumi,
have been appropriated by the Ismailis into their tradition. This
spiritual affinity is demonstrated in the following lines by Rumi:

> The sovereign of wisdom and religion was Ali,
> the one prostrating to God and prostrated to by
> the angels was Ali.

> The light-spreading sun and king of the two worlds,
> the moon in the sphere of gift and generosity
> was Ali.[13]

It was not until the tenth/sixteenth century when Shi'ism became
widespread in Persia under the Shi'i Safawid dynasty that the Ismailis
were able to declare their religious allegiance openly and emerge once

again as an organized community. The Ismailis were now reunited with their Imams, who established their residence in central Iran and were able to communicate with their followers in Syria, India and Central Asia as far as the borders of China. At the same time, there was a revival of Ismaili thought and literature in Persian, which is notable for the importance it gave to poetry as a medium of religious discourse. This partiality for poetry was, to a certain extent, dictated by the general popularization of mystical verse in Persian culture and the enormous growth of religious poetry in Twelver Shi'ism which followed the advent of the Safawids in 907/1501.

As in Fatimid literature, the poetry of post-Alamut Persian Ismailism arose directly from the activities of the rejuvenated Nizari Ismaili *da'wa*. The tradition was probably renewed by 'Abd Allah Ansari (d. 904/1498), reinforced by Khayrkhwah-i Harati (d. after 960/1553), and continued over the centuries, notably in the family of Khaki Khurasani (d. c. 1056/1646) who produced several generations of poets, including the highly talented Fida'i Khurasani who died in 1923. The Ismaili sources refer to a number of other gifted poets whose works are either lost or remain uncollected in diverse manuscripts, as in the case of Mahmud 'Ali who flourished in the eleventh/ seventeenth century, and the unfortunate Amri Shirazi who was executed by the Safawids in 999/1591 for having associated with a proscribed group of Sufis.

The resurgence of Ismaili literary life was not confined to the Persian-speaking Ismailis but extended to the communities in neighbouring regions, encouraged by a regular movement of *da'i*s to and from the headquarters of the Imams. An interesting example of the kind of cultural transference that is likely to have taken place in this period can be found in the work of the Syrian Ismaili poet, Shaykh Khudr, who is known to have visited Iran for an audience with Imam Shah Nizar in the early part of the twelfth/eighteenth century. Shaykh Khudr appears to have possessed a remarkable poetic talent with a highly innovative and imaginative style of writing. While his poetry is grounded in the metaphysical worldview of Fatimid Ismailism, a tradition partially maintained by the Syrian Ismailis after the end of

Fatimid rule in Egypt, it also exhibits a clear affinity with the mystical philosophy of post-Alamut Persian Ismailism:

> The luminous full-moon
> is the night's cupbearer;
> at his coming, the darkness
> vanishes, like a fugitive slave.
>
> Familiarity can find
> nothing but kindness from
> him, as if his sanctuary
> were the icon of a monk.
>
> Short in stature and
> hidden in substance,
> he aspires to the human
> with the passion of desire.
>
> He crosses the gardens
> crowned with contentment,
> like a star by the side
> of a planet as it sets.

The poems of Shaykh Khudr are often complex and surrealistic in their conflation of ideas and images, as well as mystical and visionary in their use of illuminary symbolism. For these reasons, as much as for the light they shed on the Syrian Ismaili community in the period of Ottoman rule, they deserve serious study.

Perhaps the most intensive process of cross-cultural fertilization in Ismaili history was demonstrated by the Ismaili *da'wa* in the Indian subcontinent. The earliest Ismaili communities there were founded in north-western India by Fatimid *da'is* sent from Egypt in the fourth/tenth century. There followed a period of revival and consolidation of the community in the ninth/fifteenth century, particularly in Kashmir, Panjab, Sind and Gujarat. According to local traditions, the spread of Ismailism was spearheaded by a long series of Persian *da'is* or *pirs* and their successors, whose teachings were conducted almost entirely through oral instruction and devotional hymns which are attributed to them. A large number of these poems were preserved as an oral tradition for several centuries before they began to be collected and recorded under the generic name of *ginan*, a term of Sanskrit origin meaning knowledge or wisdom.

The complex origins, authorship, transmission and recording of the *ginan*s have been subjected to intense research by Ismaili and other scholars in recent years.[14] Clearly, the eclectic and syncretic nature of the *ginan*s cannot be understood outside the particular features of medieval Indo–Muslim culture. The spread of Ismailism was part of a much larger advance of Islam throughout the Indian subcontinent that was spearheaded by Sufi orders and a regular influx of poets, writers and thinkers from Persia. The intensive cultural interface of Islam and local religious cultures led to the growth of a substantial body of popular religious poetry in the vernacular that intermingled Sufi and Bhakti elements, and was often shared by various local groups, including the Ismailis, as a collective folk tradition.

The Ismaili poetic literature, whether in Arabic, Persian or Indic languages, is generally of limited value as a source of information about the history, doctrines or liturgy of the community at particular times and places. But as is well known in the field of cultural anthropology, the poetic tradition of a people can provide useful insights into their perceptions of social reality and their self-image in relation to others. If Ismaili poetry is thus conceived as an expression of shared communal experience, then it must reflect the fundamental structures of that experience. The uncovering of these patterns and relationships, especially through phenomenological and structuralist modes of enquiry, can help to shed new light on the development of Ismaili religious life and thought.

Indeed, it is by way of the intrinsic study of Ismaili poetry that we may be able to address one of the central questions that has engaged modern scholars in Ismaili studies. Given that the Ismailis have always been a minority community of Islam, often subject to political and religious persecution and unable to practise their faith openly, what was it that enabled them to preserve their individuality and integrity as Ismailis? How were they able to sustain their identity and consciousness through the vicissitudes of history?[15] In this connection, the Ismaili poetic tradition must surely represent a primary area of investigation because of its pivotal role in the formation of various Ismaili communities and as a continuing source of inspiration in their spiritual life to the present day.

This publication is a compilation of some of the shorter poems and verses of the leading Ismaili poets who composed in Arabic or Persian. It does not include a sample of devotional poetry from the Indian subcontinent, nor of the substantial poetic literature of the Ismailis in Tajistikan which has become accessible only recently and is largely in manuscript form. In selecting, translating and interpreting the poems, the aim has been to convey the spirit of Ismaili poetic sensibility in a manner accessible to both the general and the specialist reader in modern English, and in accordance with some of the poetic conventions of the English language. The anthology also contains brief biographical accounts of the poets, as well as explanatory endnotes which are confined mainly to allusions and references to the Qur'an, the *hadith*, and technical terms used by the poets.

NOTES

1. The most comprehensive account of Ismailism and developments in Ismaili studies is provided by Farhad Daftary in his *The Isma'ilis: Their History and Doctrines* (Cambridge, 1990). The standard bibliographical surveys of Ismaili literature are by Ismail K. Poonawala, *Biobibliography of Isma'ili Literature* (Malibu, Ca., 1977), and W. Ivanow, *Ismaili Literature: A Bibliographical Survey* (Tehran, 1963).
2. On the beginnings of religious poetry in Islam and the Prophet's attitude to poetry in general, see Gustave von Grunebaum, "The Early Development of Islamic Religious Poetry", *Journal of the American Oriental Society*, 60 (1940), pp. 23–9; Francesco Gabrieli, "Religious Poetry in Early Islam", in G.E.von Grunebaum, ed., *Arabic Poetry: Theory and Development* (Wiesbaden, 1973), pp. 5–17; and James A. Bellamy, "The Impact of Islam on Early Arabic Poetry", in Alford T. Welch and Pierre Cachia, eds, *Islam: Past Influence and Present Challenge* (Edinburgh, 1979), pp. 141–67.
3. A succinct review of the religio-political verses of the early Shi'i and Khariji movements in the time of the Umayyads and early 'Abbasids is given by Salma K. Jayyusi, "Umayyad Poetry", in A.F.L. Beeston et al., eds, *The Cambridge History of Arabic Literature: Arabic Literature to the End of the Umayyad Period* (Cambridge, 1983), pp. 387–432, and R. Rubinacci, "Political Poetry", in Julia Ashtiany et al., eds, *The Cambridge*

Introduction

History of Arabic Literature: 'Abbasid Belles-Lettres (Cambridge, 1990),
pp. 185–201. See also Wilferd Madelung, "The 'Hashimiyyat' of al-
Kumayt and Hashimi Shi'ism", in his *Religions and Ethnic Movements
in Medieval Islam* (London, 1992), article V.

4. For a general account of the development of Islamic religious and
mystical poetry, see Annemarie Schimmel, *As Through a Veil: Mystical
Poetry in Islam* (New York, 1982).

5. An English translation of the *Kitab al-tawasin* appears in Louis
Massignon's monumental and penetrating study, *The Passion of Mansur
al-Hallaj: Mystic and Martyr of Islam*, tr. Herbert Mason (Princeton,
1982), vol.3, pp. 279–327.

6. The development of poetry in honour and praise of the Prophet is ex-
amined by Annemarie Schimmel in her *And Muhammad is His Messen-
ger: The Veneration of the Prophet in Islamic Piety* (Chapel Hill, NC,
1985), especially pp. 176–215.

7. On the connection between Shi'ism and Sufism see Henry Corbin,
History of Islamic Philosophy, tr. L. Sherrard (London, 1993), pp. 28–
30, 188–90; Seyyed Hossein Nasr, "Shi'ism and Sufism: Their Relation-
ship in Essence and in History", in his *Sufi Essays* (New York, 1977),
pp. 104–120; and J.B.Taylor, "Ja'far al-Sadiq, Spiritual Forbear of the
Sufis", *Islamic Culture*, 40 (1966), pp. 97–113.

8. S.M. Stern, "Ja'far ibn Mansur al-Yaman's Poems on the Rebellion of
Abu Yazid", in his *Studies in Early Isma'ilism* (Jerusalem–Leiden, 1983),
pp. 146–152; H.Corbin and M. Mu'in, eds. *Commentaire de la qasida
ismaélienne d'Abu'l-Haitham Jorjani* (Tehran–Paris, 1955).

9. On aspects of Fatimid poetry, see the following articles by Pieter Smoor:
"Fatimid Poets and the 'Takhallus' that Bridges the Nights of Time to
the Imam of the Time", *Der Islam*, 68 (1991), pp. 232–62; "Wine, Love
and Praise for the Fatimid Imam, the Enlightened of God", *Zeitschrift
der Deutschen Morgenländischen Gesellschaft*, 142 (1992), pp. 90–104, and
"The Poet's House: Fiction and Reality in the Works of the Fatimid
Poets", *Quaderni di Studi Arabi*, 10 (1992–93), pp. 45–62.

10. The most recent translations of Nasir-i Khusraw's poems in English are
by Annemarie Schimmel, *Make a Shield from Wisdom: Selected Verses
from Nasir-i Khusraw's Divan* (London, 1993), and Peter Lamborn
Wilson and Gholam Reza Aavani, *Nasir-i Khusraw: Forty Poems from
the Divan* (Tehran, 1977). See also E.G. Browne, *A Literary History of
Persia, from Firdawsi to Sa'di* (Cambridge, 1906), pp. 218–46.

11. The origins and dissemination of these imaginative narratives are inves-
tigated in detail by Farhad Daftary in his *The Assassin Legends: Myths
of the Isma'ilis* (London, 1994).

12. See Mahmud-i Shabistari, *Gulshan-i raz*, ed. and tr. E.H. Whinfield
(London, 1880), and the comments of Corbin, *Islamic Philosophy*, p. 95,
and Ivanow, *Ismaili Literature*, p. 130.

13. Jalal al-Din Rumi, *Kulliyyat-i Shams Tabrizi* (Lucknow, 1930), vol.1, p. 219.

14. For a discussion of the historical and cultural matrix of the *ginan*s, see Azim Nanji, *The Nizari Isma'ili Tradition in the Indo-Pakistan Subcontinent* (Delmar, NY, 1978); Christopher Shackle and Zawahir Moir, *Ismaili Hymns from South Asia: An Introduction to the Ginans* (London, 1992), which includes a selection of the poems in translation; as well as Ali Asani, "The Ginan Literature of the Ismailis of Indo-Pakistan: Its Origins, Characteristics and Themes', in Diana L. Eck and François Mallison, eds, *Devotion Divine: Bhakti Traditions from the Regions of India* (Gröningen–Paris, 1991), pp. 1–18, and "The Ismaili Ginans as Devotional Literature", in R.S. McGregor, ed., *Devotional Literature in South Asia* (Cambridge, 1992), pp. 101–12.

15. See, for instance, Ivanow's introduction to his *Ismaili Literature*, pp. 1–16.

Al-Qadi al-Nuʿman

Abu Hanifa al-Nuʿman b. Muhammad, otherwise known as al-Qadi al-Nuʿman, was one of the most distinguished Ismaili thinkers and writers of the Fatimid period. Born around 290/903 in Qayrawan, North Africa, he entered the service of the first Fatimid caliph, Imam al-Mahdi, in 313/925. In a long and illustrious career, he served four Fatimid caliphs, first as keeper of the palace library, then as judge in Tripoli and Mansuriyya, and finally as chief judge in Cairo during the time of Imam al-Muʿizz. Al-Qadi al-Nuʿman, who died in 363/974, was the author of numerous works on the Ismaili system of law under the Fatimids, as well as books on history, theology, philosophy, and some poetry. The introductory poem is from his celebrated *qasida* known as *al-Urjuza al-mukhtara*, ed. Ismail K. Poonawala (Montreal, 1970).

THE MOST HIGH

Praise be to God, how marvellous is His creation,
without an example of anything preceding it!
Indeed, it is He who preceded all things
and originated them by the command of His will.

He took neither a wife nor a son to Himself,
nor is there anyone with a likeness to Him;
nor has He a *wazir* from His creatures,
nor an associate or assistant to help Him.

Far exalted is He to be compared to
a majestic king, for He is beyond analogy,
and similitude, beyond the limits of description,
attributes, opinions and estimations of direction.

He is the One whom the eyes cannot see,
He is the One whom no region can embrace.
The intellect cannot comprehend His knowledge,
nor has He a counterpart or an equal.

He is the Most High and the Most Blessed.
There's not a thing that can be compared to Him.
Thus is He adored, besought and worshipped:
the Unified, the Glorified and the Praised!

Ibn Hani al-Andalusi

Muhammad ibn Hani al-Andalusi was one of the foremost Arabic poets of his time, whose verses were widely admired in the Arab world and earned him the title of "Mutanabbi of the West". He was born in Seville, educated in Cordova and became famous throughout Muslim Spain for his poetry. But soon his verses incurred the hostility of the anti-Ismaili Umayyad rulers and he was compelled to leave for North Africa where he offered his services to the Fatimid military commander, Jawhar al-Siqilli. When his poetic talents became recognized, he was appointed the official court poet of the Fatimid caliph, Imam al-Mu'izz. Ibn Hani died mysteriously, probably murdered by 'Abbasid or Umayyad agents, while he was on his way to Egypt from North Africa in 362/973. The selection of his poems is from *Tabyin al-ma'ani fi sharh diwan Ibn Hani al-Andalusi*, ed. Zahid 'Ali (Cairo, 1933).

A SHIMMERING LIGHT

All things exist due to
a cause: the world was
created for him and to
him belong all creatures.

His home is the pure
water of revelation,
which comes gushing forth
from a healing pool.

It is the thicket of
paradise where the fruits
ripen and to which
the shadows return.

It is the flame of
the firebrand seen by
Moses when he was
thrust in the darkness.[1]

It is the mine of
spiritual sanctity,
the essence of which
is a shimmering light.

Ibn Hani al-Andalusi

O CHILDREN OF FATIMA!

O children of Fatima![2]
              Is there in our resurrection
a means of protection for us,
              a sure refuge other than you?

You are the friends of God
              and the friends of His people,
God's pious *khalifas* and proofs,
              ever-present on the earth.[3]

You are from the people of
              prophecy, messengership and guidance,
the pure chiefs manifest
              clearly for everyone to see.

You are the people of *tanzil*
              and *ta'wil*, the expositors
of the lawful and the unlawful,
              without contradiction or rejection.[4]

Indeed, if you were to strike
              a rock, a multitude of streams
would burst out of their bonds
              and pour forth in sheer abundance!

THE PROGENY OF HASHIM

When the rain came down
in torrents, it did so
on the pole and tent
that was raised by you.

And when a blessing was
offered, it was upon
the progeny of Hashim,[5]
the lords of the people.

It is they who made firm
the prop of the time,
they who restored order
when there was corruption.

A Prophet chosen to
guide by revelation,
and the Imams who
maintain peace and justice.

They are the people of
God's lake overflowing with
water that is pure, sweet,
cold and crystalline.

Do I seek anyone else
on the Day of Destruction?
Do I fear anyone but them
on the Day of Return?

When the people hastened
towards their heights,
it is because their eminence
is older than ancient 'Ad.[6]

Ibn Hani al-Andalusi

I've not seen any poem
    in praise of someone other
than you which is not full of
    disbelief or apostasy.

Indeed, you have come
    by your own choosing,
and there's nothing that can be
    added to your glory.

THE FOUNDATION OF FAITH

I saw the Imam, who is
    the foundation of faith;
obedience to him is success,
    and disobedience loss.

I count his praise
    like the praise of God,
the true submission and praise
    by which sin is forgiven.

He is the inheritor
    of the world, and to him
belong all human beings
    between the two poles.

His position is not
    acquired by insight alone,
nor is he compelled to follow
    the opinion of others.

But it is there in
    the knowledge received by
one Imam from another,
    who preserves it.

It is a treasure of
   knowledge divine, which is
derived neither from
   augury nor physiognomy[7]

THE GLORY OF OUR TIME

O Mu'izz li-Din Allah![8]
The outstanding glory
and greatness of our time
is surely due to you.

By you is the universe
honoured and allotted
its provisions, epochs
and respites of time.

When the turbid depths
were purified for you,
the waters became sweet
and mouths became fragrant.

Your qualities are beyond
the tongue's description,
beyond what the truthful
and the garrulous say.

God has bestowed on you
the book and His grace.
But alas, my verses
are not worthy of you!

Ibn Hani al-Andalusi

THE FIRST CREATION

This is my Ma'add and all creatures are below him;
this is Mu'izz the crowned, and he is our faith.[9]

This is the heart of the first creation of God,
which He commenced, unseen and hidden from all.

For him is measured what has been measured in
the Mother of the Book, and the universe created.[10]

And because of him it was that Adam received words
of forgiveness, and Jonah was shaded by a gourd plant.[11]

Had it not been for him, the loaded ark would not
have saved Noah from being overwhelmed by the flood.[12]

His house is the house of God, and it is venerated;
his light is the light of God, which is manifested.

His veil is the veil of the unseen, the hidden;
his secret is the secret of revelation, well-guarded.

You are the light and every other light is darkness;
you are the superior and all others are inferior.

If your command were to become known to a people,
they would know what is to happen before it happened.

If your joy was expressed in the rays of the sun,
its forehead would not be eclipsed at the time of rising.

God accepts our sacrifices through that which
is pleasing to you and through that which you sustain.

So grant your slaves the favour of your intercession,
and come close to us, because you are the powerful.

We praise you not that it is a matter of pride for you,
since nothing of prose or poetry is worthy of you.

What I say about you has been revealed; thus every
poem is an interpolation of what has already been said.

THE PROOF OF GOD

You run with the light of God
among His servants so that you
may illumine their hearts
and shine therein as His proof.[13]

Our eyes have observed your
brilliance, but in fact
opinion has never understood
the essence of your reality.

I fear you with a reverence,
lest the sun forgets its rising,
just as your remembrance made
the angels forget their praise.

You are the Spirit because
your image is shaped from
the spiritual world of your Lord
and supported by knowledge.

I swear that if the world did
not call you a caliph,
they would certainly have
called you a second Messiah.[14]

Ibn Hani al-Andalusi

YOU ARE THE ONE

Command what you will,
    not what the fates ordain,
for you are the one,
    the overpowering one.

You are the one, the heir
    to Muhammad's legacy,
and your helpers are like
    those who supported him.

You are the one of whom
    glad tidings were given
by learned men in their
    books and traditions.

You are the one, Imam
    of the righteous, by whom
tyranny and disbelief
    are wholly subdued.

You are the one through
    whose love and affection,
salvation is foreseen
    and our burdens removed.

You are the one on whose
    intercession we depend
when tomorrow brings forth
    the Day of Resurrection.

You are the one in whose
    presence the fire of hell
would at once flicker out
    if it were to see you.

All glory belongs to
   the progeny of Ahmad:[15]
what is not ascribed to them
   is empty of glory!

HEAVEN ON EARTH

Rouse yourself from the sleep
of negligence so that what
shines out in the morning
is not hidden from your eyes!

The heaven you see above
is not the heaven of God,
but it is the earth below
which encompasses that heaven.

The stars submit to him,
but conceal their prostration,
and the sun shields its eyelids
from the brilliance of his light.

He is the intercessor for
the community which follows him,
just as his forefathers
were for their forefathers.

He is the trusted of God
among His servants on earth,
if at all the trusted can
be counted in His country.

This is the beloved one
of the city of Mecca,
and of its mountain-paths,
its black stone and the plain.

Ibn Hani al-Andalusi

There is a sign on him
left by the Prophet's marking,
and a splendour about him
which comes from the light of God.

IF YOU WERE NOT TO BE

God has a secret about you
which, if divulged, would enable
one to restore the dead to life
by the utterance of your name.

If the books had not foretold
of your coming, the meaning
of their verses could not have
been explained to the people.

If God had not denied to His
creatures what He has given you,
there would be no need for us
to use simile or analogy.

If there had not been a veil
placed before the knowledge in you,
people would have found a way to
seek out the hidden knowledge.

If you were not to exist,
our thoughts would not caution us,
nor intellect be our guidance,
nor analogy be a precept.

If you were not the means
of salvation for the people,
their faith would not be worth even
the value of the basest coin.

If you had not enabled us to
recognize the essence of our
souls, the world would have been
altogether unknown to us.

If you were not present here,
the pillars of civilization
would collapse and human
habitations crumble to dust.

If people had no faith in you,
they would have gone astray
from the path of true guidance,
and the guide would then be no guide.

THOSE WHO HAVE LOST THEIR WAY

I am amazed at the people who have lost
their way while God has made the guidance clear.

They did not perceive the truth when it appeared,
nor did they see the dawn when it arrived.

Guidance was not hidden from them, but it was
slavery to passion that misled their intellects.

There is not a nation on earth created in vain,
nor a people left without the help of God.[16]

We obey an Imam who obeys God and is invested
by Him with the command of what He wills.

The decree forgives those whom he forgives,
and death assails those whom he assails.

After him, there's no wall of the Ka'ba to visit;
before him, there's no other point to be led to.

Ibn Hani al-Andalusi

THE PILGRIMAGE OF A MOUNT

A caravan of fine camels performed the pilgrimage with us,
across a vast waterless desert to the Imam's sacred house.

I asked myself: "Do I have permission to enter paradise?"
Indeed, I have already approached the door open before it.

He is the king who overwhelmed the exigencies of time,
humbling all that was unruly and intractable in the world.

He is the cloud from which our life pours down, not like
a moisture-laden cloud which sheds only water upon us.

He is the reviver of good fortune, and if a mortal were
to shake his hand, the hand of death would not touch him.

He came bearing with him the splendour of the sword
Dhu'l-faqar, as if he were adorned with its belt.[17]

To him has been given the excellence of the caliphate;
to him has been vouchsafed the secret of inspiration.

O you blessed with contentment, the *khalifa* of God!
O you whose path, minaret and book are in agreement!

O the best of those to whom a mount has made pilgrimage!
O the best of those who give plenitude as a gift!

What can I say? Your reality is beyond our knowledge,
and so neither our eloquence nor silence is of avail to us.

ENCOUNTER IN THE DESERT

What I saw with my own eyes
surpassed all that I had heard,
and I was awed by that day,
more awesome than Resurrection Day.

In the morning, the horizon
was covered by another like it,
and the sun turned around to
set from where it was rising.

When I greeted Jawhar, I did
not know how to accompany him,
nor when I accompanied him
how to bid farewell to him.[18]

How could I have penetrated
the army when it was like
a vast ocean and I was
fascinated by its commander?

When I rose for his farewell,
he had already departed;
then I swore that no bed
would rest my side again.

It was dark when I reached
the pavilion, and I aspired
to him while the torches
were lifted above our heads.

Their light pierced the bosom
of the moisture-laden clouds,
and set fire to the waves of
the black and brown ocean.

So I spent the night there
with the army whose conversation
kept me awake while the *jinns*[19]
slept peacefully in the desert.

THUNDER IN THE MOUNTAINS

Beware that this great army
is the multitude of one whose
eyelids have never tasted sleep
nor slept a night quietly.

His goodwill for the country
has blocked my path, and there's not
the distance of a finger
between the length of two spears.

When they saw it, the mountains
became submissive: what then
of human hearts which are
by nature even more submissive?

There's not been an army before
such as Jawhar's in which
the mounts have pressed onwards
for ten full days without stopping.

Every movement of its advance
makes the solid mountains move,
and by a slight tremor, to
bow and prostrate before it.

When it alights, the land is
transformed into cities, but when
it departs, the land returns to
what it was, a buried wasteland.

ASSEMBLY OF BANNERS

A roaring thunder echoed
at the end of the night,
and flashing lightning appeared
with the coming of the dawn.

And from the terror inspired
by that sound, wild animals
revealed to us what God had
ordained for you and for us.

And the birds hovering above
were seized by fear, not
knowing where to take refuge
or from whom to seek asylum.

Until there appeared the sword
of the Hashimite empire,
on whose face is shining
a light emanating from God.[20]

The shadows of the banners
assembled before him are
like the clouds of divine help
which never break or disperse.

And the unsheathed swords,
when they sweep over the land,
are like the rise and swell
of a vast, overflowing ocean.

Amir Tamim al-Fatimi

Prince Tamim was the eldest son of the fourth Fatimid caliph, Imam al-Mu'izz li-Din Allah. He was born in 337/948–9 in Mahdiyya, the first Fatimid capital in North Africa. At the age of 25, he was one of those who accompanied his father on his historic journey to Egypt, when the seat of the Fatimid government was transferred to Cairo. The prince was generally averse to political life and dedicated himself to literary and cultural pursuits until his premature death in 374/984. Amir Tamim's poems are from his *Diwan*, ed. M.H. al-A'zami et al. (Cairo, 1957).

ELEGY FOR AL-MU'IZZ

How can bodies not
  lose their hearts if
their faces have all
  turned pale with grief?

Who will now console
  the magnanimous ones?
Who will bring comfort
  to the sorrowful throne?

After you, they have
  lost their hearts whose
tearing from the breast
  was incumbent upon them.

O Mu'izz! O Mu'izz![21]
  Until the tears which
stream from my eyes
  become fertile with blood:

Let someone other
  than me taste this life,
because without you,
  there's no merit in it.

Amir Tamim al-Fatimi

ON THE FESTIVAL OF NAWRUZ

When I compose a poem in praise of you,
I feel inspired and my speech becomes refined.

But if I wish to praise someone other than you,
I'm tongue-tied and my speech disproves the lie.

Because you are born for grace and eminence,
and such gifts are indeed innate to your nature,

your honour is the dawn, your face a bright star,
and your right hand pours rain upon the creation.

You are the light from which we seek illumination,
the gracious beloved for whom ransom is given.

Through you, our days of tyranny turn to order,
and the indomitable, treacherous time is humbled.

If Nawruz is a festival of joy and delight,[22]
it is through your light that it has come to be so.

So live long! Bring glory and prosperity to the times;
if they do not prosper by you, may they be ruined!

O son of the Prophet, God's blessings be on you!
You are a time-tested sword to fight life's sorrows.

TIME AND DESTINY

O time! How come that my destiny
has been cut asunder from you?
Why have you so ruined my strength that
it lies blind and broken before you,
its fragments beyond repair?

Time has grown old, weak and wretched,
afflicted by the negligence of age;
it has become more impotent than
a corpse, more remote than death,
more silent than a lute without string.

Time was once more aggressive to us;
it was more violent than a lion
leaping upon grazing livestock,
lustier than a woman when she
is deprived of the company of man.

If it had not been for 'Aziz,[23]
the trustee of God, my soul would
never have turned to seek refuge from
the vagaries of time, nor would it
have found sanctuary with him.

Al-Mu'ayyad fi'l-Din al-Shirazi

A prolific writer, poet, theologian, political and military organizer, al-Mu'ayyad fi'l-Din al-Shirazi was one of the leading figures of the Fatimid government under Imam al-Mustansir, the eighth Fatimid caliph. Born around 390/1000 in Shiraz, Persia, al-Mu'ayyad first rose to prominence in the local Buwayhid court where he converted the ruler and many of his courtiers and commanders to Ismailism. This aroused the hostility of the 'Abbasids, as a result of which he went into exile. After a long and dangerous journey, al-Mu'ayyad reached Cairo in 438/1046, where he served the cause of the Fatimids in various political, military and religious capacities. For several years, he was actively involved in directing the military campaign which led to the establishment of Fatimid suzerainty over Baghdad briefly in 450/1058. In the same year, he was appointed the administrative head of the Ismaili *da'wa* and its academic institution, the Dar al-'Ilm, where he continued to lecture until his death in 470/1078. The following poems are from his *Diwan*, ed. Muhammad K. Husayn (Cairo, 1949).

THE PURE PROGENY

Peace be upon the pure progeny,
and welcome to their resplendent lights.

I begin with peace upon Adam from whom
came all mankind, whether nomadic or sedentary.

Peace be upon the one whose flood made
the reprobates suffer from great misfortune.

Peace be upon the one to whom came
the peace at dawn when he was engulfed by fire.

Peace be upon the one who with his staff
overpowered the unbelievers of the tyrant Pharaoh.

Peace be upon Jesus, the Holy Spirit,
who by his coming, bestowed honour on Nazareth.

Peace be upon Ahmad, the chosen,
the one who intercedes in the hereafter.

Peace be upon Haydar, the beloved,[24]
and those descended from him, the radiant stars.

Peace be upon you, O sovereign-lord
of Cairo, and all their gain abides with you.

I sacrifice my soul to Mustansir,[25]
who is supported by the legions of heaven.

I bear witness that it is your blessed face
which illumines the faces of your followers.

You are the custodian of the fountain of life,
and may the fountain of your enemies perish!

Al-Mu'ayyad fi'l-Din al-Shirazi

THE EVIL OF DESIRE

Alas, my intellect
has become oppressed
and defeated by
the evil of desire.

Woe to me because
I have wronged myself.
I am beyond neither
blame nor reproach.

O why did I waste
my life when the path
of guidance was open
and spacious to me?

And why did I lose
the light by which
I am related to
the close and noble ones?

Why do I debase
the precious pearl
and honour the mean
and insignificant oyster?

THE SOUL'S SATISFACTION

O Thursday morning,[26]
    welcome be to you!
  May the Protector,
    the One, increase
      His favours to you.

You are indeed
  a venerable festival
    for the believers,
      whose faith has
        reunited them in you.

Whenever Thursday
  approaches and passes,
    we hasten to pluck
      the fruits which grow
        in the garden of Eden.

The gardens where
  flow the streams of
    pure pristine water,
      and the pure maidens
        appear in the palaces.

The water which is
  more sweet and healing
    than cool water, and
      brings satisfaction
        to the thirsty soul.[27]

Al-Mu'ayyad fi'l-Din al-Shirazi

THE LIGHT OF INTELLECT

How many observers are there
  with eyes that cannot see?
How many seers are there
  with hearts that cannot reflect?

For the human eye to see,
  there are certain conditions;
he who disregards them
  loses his way in the darkness.

The eye is of no avail
  if it does not receive light
from the sun or the moon,
  or from a burning torch.

Similarly the intellect,
  during reflection by itself,
remains in the throes of
  doubt and bewilderment.

Except when it is helped
  by a light from outside;
then it ascends the ladder
  of enlightened contemplation.

THE SANCTUARY

Run to the sanctuary of the safe house,
which is surrounded by bliss and prosperity.

His exposition of revelation is aided
by his understanding of its hidden meanings.

And his interpretation of the law is
adorned by the lucidity of his reasoning.

He brings souls out of their darkness
and draws out fruits from their outer skin.

You see him as the rising sun of clarity
and as the river of abundant bounty.

By his brilliant wisdom, hearts are cured,
and by his copious mercy, they are revived.

He manifests himself in every age,
and creatures are not guided except by him.

His mission is established in the world,
exalted with signs clear and recognizable.

He certainly is Mustansir, the triumphant,[28]
the one by whom everything becomes prosperous.

He is the best of Fatima's progeny,
the scion of Zahir and the grandson of Hakim.

He is God's mercy on his servants
and the mine of provisions in the hereafter.

I have composed a poem about him,
like a necklace of pearls and gems strung together.

Nasir-i Khusraw

Nasir-i Khusraw is acknowledged as one of the foremost poets of the Persian language. Born in the Balkh district of Central Asia in 394/ 1004, Nasir was inspired from an early age by a tremendous thirst for knowledge. His intellectual abilities brought him much fame, a promising career in government service, and a life of ease and pleasure. But he was always dissatisfied by a lack of meaning and purpose in his life until one day, at the age of 42, he was dramatically transformed by a visionary dream. He converted to Ismailism, renounced his worldly life and embarked on his famous seven-year journey to Egypt. Nasir arrived in Cairo in 439/1047, where he stayed for three years and became acquainted with Ismaili dignitaries such as al-Mu'ayyad fi'l-Din al-Shirazi. He was appointed to a high rank in the Fatimid *da'wa* organization, and was later regarded as the *hujja* of greater Khurasan. When he returned to Transoxania, Nasir established his residence at Balkh, from where he began to propagate the Ismaili faith in the surrounding provinces. But Nasir's success provoked the local people to burn down his house and compel him to seek refuge in Yumgan, a remote mountainous region of Badakhshan, today situated on both sides of the Oxus river in Tajikistan and Afghanistan. Nasir spent the remainder of his life there, writing his philosophical works and composing poetry until his death after 465/1072. He is venerated to this day in Central Asia as a great saint, poet and philosopher. The following poems are from his *Diwan*, ed. N. Taqawi (Tehran, 1925–28), also edited by M. Minuwi and M. Muhaqqiq (Tehran, 1974).

THE PROPHET'S FAITH

I have chosen the Qur'an
    and the faith of Muhammad,
because they were the ones
    chosen by Muhammad.

Surely, if I follow
    them both, my certainty
will become strong and steadfast
    like that of Muhammad.

My key to paradise,
    my guide to delight,
my impregnable fortress
    is the faith of Muhammad.

Muhammad was sent to us
    as the Messenger of God:
thus was inscribed on
    the seal-ring of Muhammad.

The Qur'an and the faith
    live in our hearts, just as
they used to dwell in
    the heart of Muhammad.

By the grace of God, I pray
    that I will become
amongst the most humble
    followers of Muhammad.

IN SEARCH OF KNOWLEDGE

The Prophet said,
"Seek knowledge in China";[29]
so I set out for that China of Muhammad.

There I heard
from the Prophet's heir
sweet discourses like the honey of Muhammad.

From the son
of Haydar and Zahra,[30]
I took the upright character of Muhammad.

From that son,
renowned in the world,
came to me the sublime eminence of Muhammad.

I would not
have received more grace
than this had I lived in the time of Muhammad.

The Creator of
the world has blessed me
with the love of 'Ali and the praise of Muhammad.

Now I am,
with the blessing of God,
secure in the impregnable fortress of Muhammad.

I seek help
from Muhammad in the east:
what seek you from me who seeks the help of Muhammad?

THE PROPHET'S LEGACY

Listen, O brothers! In the ocean of faith,
the Qur'an is the most precious pearl of Muhammad.
Just as every king keeps his treasure concealed,
the Qur'an is the hidden treasure of Muhammad.

Observe well, who do you see as the custodian
of this treasure and the trustee of Muhammad?
Just as you leave your treasure to your children,
there is a legacy for the children of Muhammad.

Do you not see that the pearls of faith cannot
come from anyone except the children of Muhammad?
This treasure was entrusted to one person only,
worthy of being the confidant of Muhammad.

He was none other than the Prophet's dear friend,
whose spouse was the pure daughter of Muhammad,
the lady of paradise: from them were born
Husayn and Hasan, the *sin* and *shin* of Muhammad.[31]

I am certain that in both the worlds, Husayn
and Hasan are the rose and jasmine of Muhammad.
Tell me, where in the world can blossom such
exquisite blooms except in the soil of Muhammad?

I can never bring myself to choose anyone over
and above these two beloved sons of Muhammad.
If I were to desire someone else in their place,
how disgraced will I be in the presence of Muhammad!

Nasir-i Khusraw

THE SWORD OF 'ALI

The Qur'an and the pure
    sword of Haydar – these are
the two foundations of
    the faith of Muhammad.

For he, 'Ali, stood with
    his sword Dhu'l-faqar,[32]
drawn in every battle on
    the right hand of Muhammad.

'Ali's rank in the faith
    was like Aaron to Moses,[33]
for he was both the peer
    and companion of Muhammad.

On the Day of Resurrection,
    Aaron and Moses will kiss
the mantle of 'Ali and
    the sleeve of Muhammad.

Muhammad's religion was
    like a dense forest;
'Ali was the lion in
    the forest of Muhammad.

THE EXCELLENCE OF 'ALI

The springtime of a friend of 'Ali
is always full of the efflorescence of 'Ali.
None deserves eminence and praise among
the people except he who befriends 'Ali.

The heart of every Shi'i is protected
from Satan in the fortress of 'Ali.
As 'Ali is from the Prophet's family,
the true Shi'i belongs to the family of 'Ali.

A hundred years of praise is not equal
to even one in a thousand praises of 'Ali.
Courage, knowledge, abstinence, generosity:
these are the qualities I revere in 'Ali.

Therefore, my back is bent with gratitude
under the weight of the favours of 'Ali.
My under and outer garments are faith
and knowledge, just as they were for 'Ali.

If you want to understand his status,
reflect upon the role and deeds of 'Ali:
he was a lion, the battlefield his meadow,
and Gabriel was the spearman of 'Ali.

'Ali's cave is of knowledge, not stone,
for stone does not befit the glory of 'Ali.
The clouds of *ta'wil* do not shed their droplets
except on the trees and seed-fields of 'Ali.[34]

'Ali had no desire for gold or silver;
faith and knowledge were the choice of 'Ali.
There was no fault in him nor blemish in
the tongue, hands and garments of 'Ali.

Husayn and Hasan, the Prophet's reminders,
were none other than the reminders of 'Ali.
Truly no one can be saved from the fire
unless he comes under the protection of 'Ali.

O PEOPLE OF THE UMMA!

O people of the *umma*!
I'm bewildered by your ignorance
and misfortune, which have
made you the Prophet's enemy.

If I said that 'Ali is
the successor of the Prophet,
why have I become prey to
the punishment due for evil?

They accuse me of that which
is my pride and honour, the fact
that I became a follower
of the people of the cloak.[35]

They have driven me from my home
for the sake of religion; thus
have I suffered in migration
like the Messenger of God.

The star of Alcor is well-known
but obscure on the horizon;
I have become invisible
like Alcor on the earth.

Thanks be to God that,
due to His grace, I command
the lives and the substance of
the believers in Yumgan.

Since the prince of believers
bade me welcome, I have
drawn close to the faithful
through the door of his greetings.

I have not stood before
anyone other than the Creator
of the world, nor bowed down
to anyone other than God.

Now the free men of the world
seek my company because
I have become the chosen
of 'Ali, the favourite of God.

Ahmad entrusted his banner
to 'Ali; therefore I seek
refuge under the blessed
and exalted banner of 'Ali.

THE WORLD'S FRIENDSHIP

O do not make business with this world
which takes from you a cloak for a needle!

I sought its company but found no profit
from it because it wore me down.

If you cannot escape its friendship,
how can you be liberated from yourself?

Woe to the one who is imprisoned by himself!
May he be bankrupt in both the worlds!

This world is the internment of hearts:
throw away the trapdoor from your heart!

Your abode is not here but in another
world which is brilliant and everlasting.

Nasir-i Khusraw

THE EYE OF THE INTELLECT

O young man! Arise from
   the sleep of negligence
and look upon the world with
   the keen eye of intellect!

O ignorant one! Why do you
   waste your time sleeping
and eating, for that is
   the work of a donkey?

Have you ever thought why
   God has given you intellect?
That you may eat and sleep
   contentedly like a donkey?

If the ear of your
   conscience had not been deaf,
you would have heard the praise
   of the seven spheres.[36]

If you do not reach out
   to grasp the Hand of God,
you will be struck by remorse
   and suffer the penalty.

What you need is a new eye[37]
   and a fresh ear so that
you may then experience
   the great Kingdom of God.

To be sure, He will not
   grant you an audience there,
if you do not take with you
   an eye and an ear from here.

Do you not see that God
  is inviting you to heaven?
Why do you throw yourself
  into the pit of hell-fire?

In order to ascend to
  the abode of the righteous,
make knowledge your feet
  and obedience your wings.

In the battleground of
  our demented world,
make a sword from patience
  and a shield from the faith.

Pluck the bud of wisdom
  from the branch of religion;
graze the hyacinth of obedience
  from the fields of knowledge.

This world is not the abode
  of people who are wise;
it is but a passage for us;
  therefore traverse it.

Of what use is the branch
  which yields no fruit,
whether it belongs to
  a fruit-bearing tree or not?

In the sight of God,
  the Absolute Sovereign,
this world has not the value
  of even an atom.

Had it any value in His
  reckoning, do you think
the unbelievers would get
  even one sip of water?

This world is only a place
of attainment for us;
therefore gather quickly
provisions for the Return.[38]

In fact, this world is
a book in which you see
inscribed the writings
of God the Almighty.

O do not reject these
allusions of the *hujja*,[39]
because truth should never
become an abomination.

JOURNEY TO THE LIGHT

My heart is filled with the slander of the people; I am
  therefore separated from them in speech and action.

As long as my heart was blind like that of Zayd and Amr,[40]
  no one could find fault in me, wherever I went.

Sometimes burning with passion I followed beautiful maidens;
  sometimes out of greed I sought the philosopher's stone,

I did not fear that my life was being wasted, nor was I
  ashamed that I had vulgar or evil thoughts.

During autumn my heart was dissipated with wine; in the
  springtime I happily looked for water and pasture.

Complacently I sat in the midst of the watermill turning,
  until the hair on my head turned white as snow.

I thought that the world had become my meadow, until like
  the cattle I became fodder for the world.

If it injured me in any way, I returned to it yet again like
    a drunkard always drawn towards goblets of wine.

The world kept me firmly under its control; thus sometimes
    I became prosperous and sometimes a pauper.

And when my soul was worn out with the afflictions of time,
    I went to the door of the king to bestow praise on him.

I was prepared to seek justice from the devil of the time,
    but all I found in the king's service was enslavement.

I had to perform a hundred acts of servitude to him before
    I was able to fulfil even a single hope of mine.

I gained nothing at all except toil and suffering from
    the one to whom I had gone for the sake of healing.

When my heart became disappointed with kings and princes,
    I turned to the people of the mantle, turban and cloak.

I told myself that they would show me the path of religion
    because the people of the world had tormented my heart.

They said: "Be happy, you have been delivered from your burden";
    so my soul became happy and I prayed along with them.

I told myself that since these were men of knowledge, I would
    be released from the grip of ignorance and poverty.

Therefore I wasted some years of my life with them in a lot
    of empty prattle and useless disputations.

But their wealth and piety was only corruption and hypocrisy,
    and I said: "O God, why have I become afflicted again?"

It was as if by going from the king to the jurist, I had
    entered a dragon's mouth for fear of an ant!

Time had countless ruses and pretexts to entrap me; I became
    caught in just such a pretext, such a deception.

When it betrayed me and no escape was left to me, at last
    I went to the progeny of Mustafa for help.[41]

I found help against the devil's persecution and cunning
  when I entered the sanctuary of the Imam of mankind.

Shall I tell you what happened to me when I fled the devil?
  Suddenly I found myself in the company of angels.

When the light of the Imam shone upon my soul, even though
  I was black as night, I became the shining sun.

The Supreme Name is with the Imam of the time; through him,
  Venus-like, I ascended to the heavens.[42]

SPEECH AND SILENCE

O eloquent one! Why do you remain silent?
Why do you not string pearls and corals together?

If you are a rider on the mount of wisdom,
why do you not come to the racecourse of men?

You have seen and experienced the world;
You have heard the sayings of Arabs and Persians.

You have become famous in the science of geometry,
from Sind and India to the borders of Khurasan.

And when you are counting, the created world is
like a grain of wild rue in your thinking.

There are many people in the east and the west
who have witnessed your claim to this science.

Now that you are happy to be among the best,
you should have pride over your fellow men,

since from the heart of the master Mu'ayyad,[43]
God has opened the door of wisdom to you.

THE MASTER AND THE DISCIPLE

The master turned
my night into broad daylight
with proofs as clear as
radiant sunlight.

Since he made me
drink from the water of life,
death has become quite
insignificant to me.

When I looked
from the corner of his eye,
I saw the earth rotating
beneath my feet.

He showed me
the visible and hidden worlds,
both located in one place,
my own body.

I saw the two
guardians of paradise and hell[44]
inhabiting the same place,
my own breast.

He pointed to one
who is the keeper of paradise
and said to me: "I am
his disciple."

I saw eight gates,
closed in the same place,
and seven other gates open,
one above the other.[45]

He said to me:
"If you wish to enter a gate,
you have to obtain his
permission first."

When I asked him
to explain the secret to me,
he recited its story from
beginning to end.

The master said:
"He is the lord of the time,
chosen by God from
men and *jinns*."[46]

THE CANDLE OF INTELLECT

Kindle the candle of intellect in your heart
    and hasten with it to the world of brightness;
If you want to light a candle in your heart,
    make knowledge and goodness its wick and oil.

In the path of the hereafter, one should not walk
    on foot but with the soul and the intellect,
and for provisions, you must fill the tablecloth
    of your heart with obedience and knowledge.

O son, your mind is the garden of intellect,
    turn it not into a furnace with fumes of wine;
your heart is the blessed mine of knowledge,
    why have you planted a perverse hardness in it?

Let your heart become soft because a shirt of
    dusky soft silk does not befit a heart of stone;
cast away ignorance from your mind because
    celebration does not befit a house of lament.

Comprehend well the wise poetry of the *hujja*,
    for it is elevated and powerful like Mount Qaran,[47]
and with the needle of reflection, prick his
    excellent words in your subtle heart and soul.

THE MOMENTUM OF TIME

O you who have been
sleeping at night!
If you have rested,
do not think that time
too has been resting.

Consider that your
personality is always
on the move – do not
think it eats or sleeps
even for a moment!

The momentum of time
and the turning sphere
draws all animals,
by night and day,
to ceaseless motion.

PEARLS OF HEAVEN

Above the seven spheres are two precious pearls whose light
illumines the world and mankind.[48]

In the placenta of non-existence, from the sperm of existence,
they form images but themselves have no form.

Not contained by the senses, they are not sensible; neither
dark nor bright, they are not visible.

Reared in pre-eternity by the holy wet-nurse, they are not
pearls but have the attributes of pearls.

From this side of creation and that side of the universe,
within and beyond time, they are always together.

They are not in the world and yet they are in it; they are not
within us but nurture the soul in our bodies.

It is said that they are both the worlds; therefore they are
in the seven climes but not in the seven climes.[49]

This one is the Holy Spirit and that one the Spirit of Gabriel;
they are flying angels but have no wings.

In the nest of the lower world they appear with open wings,
but in the higher world they fly without wings.

They are friends with the hot and the cold, the dry and the wet,
as are earth and air with fire and water.[50]

In the treasure-houses of pre-eternity and post-eternity, they are
not pearls but recognized by the name of pearl.

They are both the world and mankind, paradise and hell; they
are absent and present, poison and sugar.

They come from light to darkness, from heaven to earth, from
the west to the east, from ocean to land.

Existent and non-existent, hidden and manifest, they are
without and with you in the same house.

In the next world which is their forge and furnace, they are
the destroyers of the building and the builder.

They are the chiefs of the nine spheres and the seven planets;
they give sustenance to the five senses and the four natures.[51]

Around their home, there are ten witnesses, of whom five stay
inside and five stand at the door.[52]

The shopkeepers of heaven come before them in order to
purchase what they have to sell.

They are not substance, for substance takes accident from them;
they make an axis for accident, but they are not the axes.

They read to you the book of secrets without letters; they
know your deeds without having to see them.

They appear because they are hidden; they are without head or
body because they are in the head and body.

Their attribute is that they are not contained in the world,
but they are hidden in our head and body.

They have made this world a place for you to inhabit, but for
them there is no place, for they are beyond space.

They come to you from a place which is not a place; there they
are angels and here they are messengers.

In rank, they are higher than the angelic world; like God's
essence, they are neither element nor substance.

Even though both the worlds are in the possession of this and
that, if you wish, they can be subjugated to your soul.

Nasir-i Khusraw

THE SOVEREIGN OF TIME

The soul of the universe
is the sovereign of time,
for God has raised up
the body through the soul.

When the auspicious Jupiter
saw his face, it became
the source of munificence,
the mine of good fortune.

As long as the clouds
of Nawruz wash all quarters
of the garden with
showers of lustrous pearls;[53]

and the nightingale laments
the rose at the break of dawn,
like a grieving soul
separated from its lover:

may the authority of
the sovereign of time
prevail over space and time
and the denizens of the world!

A CONCEITED EAGLE

One day an eagle rose into the air from a rock,
his wings and feathers spread out in search of food.

He observed the broad expanse of his wings and said:
"Today the whole world is under my wingspan.

When I am soaring high, my keen eyes can see
even a particle of dust on the bottom of the sea.

And if a gnat stirs itself on a piece of straw,
my sight can behold its each and every movement."

Thus boasted the eagle without fear of fate,
but see what happened to him from the cruel sphere!

Suddenly, an arrow sped towards him, released by
a mighty archer who lay in ambush for him.

As the liver-piercing arrow struck the eagle's wing,
he plunged to the ground from a lofty height.

Sprawling in the dust, he thrashed about like a fish,
his feathers falling to the left and the right.

"How strange it is," he said, "that a piece of iron
and wood can be so swift, so hard and so piercing."

Then he saw his own feather on it and exclaimed:
"It's from me! I'm responsible for my own downfall!"

O *hujja*, cast out all conceit from your mind!
Look what happened to the eagle when he was conceited!

Nasir-i Khusraw

A PAVILION OF PARADISE

What kind of canopy is this
like an ocean full of pearls,
or as if thousands of lamps are
lit inside a burnished bowl?

If the garden were the sphere,
the tulip would be Jupiter,
and if the sphere were the garden,
the rose-bush would be Gemini.

And no one would be able to
tell the Capella from a red rose,
that the one is resplendent
and the other fragrant.[54]

See the morning as it follows
the starry Pleiades on high as if
a coral-coloured griffin has
come after a silver pheasant.[55]

It adorns the face of the east
with its many-coloured hues,
seeming as if it were
the bejewelled throne of Darius.[56]

Its myriad signs glimmer bright
in the dark revolving vault,
like an intelligent heart
dwelling in an ignorant soul.

The crescent moon would not sail
every month as a golden boat
if the rolling blue sphere
above had not been an ocean.

Nay, this is not an ocean
but a pavilion of paradise;
otherwise it would not be full
of the heavenly pure maidens.

And if someone were to say:
"If Nasir is a sage, why then
is he sitting alone like
a lonely pauper in Yumgan?"

He knows not that if I too were
to become wretched like him,
my back would also have become
bent like his before kings.

I would not like to possess
what is in the king's possession,
if the knowledge I have were
to be possessed by him instead.

How could my soul have ridden
the mount of wisdom if the one
whom I praise was not the rider
of the ash-coloured mount, Duldul?[57]

THE ESOTERIC AND THE EXOTERIC

The exoteric of revelation
    is like brackish water,
but the esoteric is like pearls
    for people who are wise.[58]

Since pearls and jewels are
    to be found on the sea-bed,
look for the pearl-diver
    instead of running on the shore.

Why does the Maintainer
   of the world keep so many
precious pearls concealed upon
   the bottom of the sea?

He kept them for the Prophet
   with the instruction:
"The esoteric is for the wise,
   the exoteric for the ignorant."

You will get nothing but mud
   and salty water from
the pearl-diver because of
   your animosity towards him.

When you are searching for
   the meaning of revelation,
do not be content with speech
   like a donkey braying aloud.

On the Night of Power,[59]
   when you kindle the lamp,
the mosque is filled with light,
   but your heart remains pitch-dark.

Whether you kindle the lamp
   or not, understand that
it will not dispel the darkness
   of ignorance in your heart.

SECRETS OF THE PILGRIMAGE

The pilgrims came with honour and reverence,
thanking God for His compassion and mercy,
having escaped the toil and trial of the Hijaz
and saved from the painful punishment of hell.[60]

They came to Mecca from 'Arafat proclaiming
"*Labbayka*! Here I am, at your service, O Lord!"
They had performed all the rites of the pilgrimage
and were now returning home, safe and healthy.

So I decided to go out and meet them, even
though it was beyond the bounds of my capacity,
because in the midst of that caravan was
a dear friend, a most sincere and noble man.

I asked him: "Tell me, how were you able
to complete such a painful and fearful journey?
Since your departure, I've had nothing except
penitence and sorrow for companionship.

I'm happy that you performed the pilgrimage,
and there's none like you in our part of the world.
But tell me, my dear friend, how did you
honour the sanctity of the great sanctuary?

When you were putting on the pilgrim's robe,
what intention did you resolve in your mind?
Did you promise yourself to make unlawful
everything other than the eternal Lord?"

He said: "No." I asked him: "Did you say
Labbayka! with full knowledge and reverence?
Did you answer God because you heard His voice
as did Moses, the interlocutor of God?"

He said: "No." I asked him: "When you stood
at 'Arafat in God's presence, did you deny
yourself and become a knower of God?
Did you feel the breeze of gnosis blow over you?"

He said: "No." I asked him: "When you slaughtered
the sheep for the sake of captives and orphans,
did you see yourself in God's proximity
and sacrifice to Him your carnal soul?"

He said: "No." I asked him: "When you went into
the sanctuary like the people of the cave,[61]
were you safe from the evil of your base self,
from the grief of parting and punishment in hell?"

He said: "No." I asked him: "When you hurled pebbles
at Satan the accursed, did you throw out
of yourself, at once and completely,
all reprehensible habits and actions?"

He said: "No." I asked him: "When you came to
know the station of Abraham, did you then
submit the whole of yourself to God with
absolute honesty, conviction and certitude?"

He said: "No." I asked him: "During the time
of circumambulation when you were trotting like
an ostrich, did you think of the circumambulation
of the angels around the Supreme Throne?"

He said: "No." I asked him: "When you ran from
Safa to Marwa in equal measure, did you
see both the worlds in the purity of your heart,
and did it become free of hell and paradise?"

He said: "No." I asked him: "Now that you are
separated from the Ka'ba, are you grief-stricken?
Did you bury yourself there as if you were
already a heap of putrefied flesh and bones?"

He said: "I have understood nothing of what
you have said, nor whether it is true or false."
I said: "Then you did not perform the pilgrimage,
nor did you reach the abode of annihilation!

You went to Mecca and returned, having purchased
only the toils of the desert for your silver.
If you want to perform the pilgrimage again,
my friend, do it in accordance with my advice."

Hasan-i Sabbah

Hasan-i Sabbah came from a Kufan family settled in the Persian town of Qum. He was educated in the nearby town of Ray and became converted to Ismailism at the age of seventeen. In 469/1076–77, Hasan was admitted to the Ismaili *da'wa* and sent for further training to Egypt where he remained for three years. On his return journey, he narrowly escaped death when his ship was wrecked off the Syrian coast. Back in Persia, Hasan travelled throughout the country which at that time was under the rule of the Seljuqs who were fiercely hostile to all Shi'is, including the Ismailis. In 483/1090, Hasan acquired control of Alamut, the first in a series of fortresses occupied by the Ismailis in northern and eastern Iran. In spite of repeated military offensives by the Seljuqs, the Ismailis managed to retain their independence until their fortresses were overcome by the Mongols in 654/1256. Hasan-i Sabbah, or "Baba Sayyidna" as he was called by the Ismailis, died in 518/1124 after an extraordinary career as an Ismaili *da'i*, a political leader, military strategist, philosopher, writer and poet. Only a few fragments of his writings have survived. The poems included here are from the *Munajat-i Baba Sayyidna*, in the *Kitab al-manaqib* (Karachi, 1986).

according to their skills, who performed an important role in court ritual and public ceremonial. The most famous of the court poets was Muhammad ibn Hani al-Andalusi who entered the service of the Fatimids in 347/958 after fleeing from anti-Ismaili persecution in Umayyad Spain. Ibn Hani was reputed as the foremost Arabic poet of the Maghrib and his poetry was widely admired by Ismailis and non-Ismailis alike from Cordova to Baghdad. As the official poet-laureate of two Imams, al-Mansur and al-Mu'izz, Ibn Hani was called upon to expound upon a variety of political, military and religious themes in support of the Fatimids. But he had a strong religious conviction and the devotional spirit runs deep through all his poetry. As the following lines demonstrate, Ibn Hani was well-versed in Ismaili thought and he was devoted to the house of the Prophet, in whose honour he composed poems of remarkable power and beauty:

> Command what you will,
>   not what the fates ordain,
> for you are the one,
>   the overpowering one...
>
> You are the one through
>   whose love and affection,
> salvation is foreseen
>   and our burdens removed.
>
> You are the one on whose
>   intercession we depend
> when tomorrow brings forth
>   the Day of Resurrection.
>
> You are the one in whose
>   presence the fire of hell
> would at once flicker out
>   if it were to see you.
>
> All glory belongs to
>   the progeny of Ahmad:
> what is not ascribed to them
>   is empty of glory!

There is scarce information about the other court poets who flourished under the patronage of the Fatimids. A large portion of their works seems to have perished in the destruction of Cairo's famed libraries

REPENTANCE

O God, O my benevolent King,
You are the Loving, the Merciful.

Forgive this weak and humble slave,
for You are the Forgiver, the Pardoner.

I confess my errors in the book
of deeds and my negligence grieves me.

I am drowned in the ocean of sin
and You know the remedy for it.

With countless sighs and lamentations,
I remain lost to Your felicity.

For I, wretched and ill-fated as I am,
could not do service worthy of my Lord.

Now from the depths of my heart I say:
"I repent! I repent! I repent!"

SUPPLICATION

I am disconcerted
by my errors;
my disgrace shames me.

Much have I gone astray;
now I will never
stray from Your door.

Hasan-i Sabbah

For me, there is no path
other than Yours,
no court other than Yours.

O Lord, by Your grace,
cast me not from
Your noble presence!

Do not drive away
Your dog when
he comes to Your door!

PARTICLES OF DUST

There is a desert in which
I have utterly lost my way;
the path is dreadful and I am
without help or companion.

I am alone and confused,
not knowing which way to go,
and thinking like this makes
my head turn with giddiness.

O my Lord! What difference
does it make between
my good and bad if both are
as particles of dust to You?

And if I were to sit or
stand improperly, accept me
as I am. O Holy One, do not
reject me, whatever I am!

MAKE ME COMPLETE

In the beginning I was non-existent
and was blissful in that nothingness;
then You removed the dust of non-being
and opened the door of existence to me.

You made the seven fathers my guardians
and the four mothers my custodians;[62]
they took me from lap to shoulder
and led me from hearing to understanding.

You gave me my soul and intellect
and from You came my heart and prudence;
then by Your grace, You caused me to
be one of the people of prostration.

You immersed me in Your merciful light
and placed on me the crown of "We honoured";[63]
my esteem was adorned by Your glory
when You established my relation with You.

Thus have I reached my present state
and never did You let me perish.
O my Lord! It is not befitting that
You should leave me half-way after this!

O God, be my guide towards Yourself
and make me proficient in my task!
O God, help me to complete my work,
and if I am incomplete, make me complete!

Ra'is Hasan

Hasan b. Salah Birjandi, also known as Ra'is Hasan, was an eminent Persian Ismaili poet and historian of the seventh/thirteenth century. The details of his life are very scarce, but it is known that he worked as a scribe and scholar for Shihab al-Din, the chief Ismaili *da'i* of Quhistan in the first half of that century. Apparently Ra'is Hasan had a considerable reputation as a poet, for his verses are quoted widely in the literary sources of later times. The poems of Ra'is Hasan shed light on the life of the Ismailis during the Alamut period. The poet died in 644/1246, some ten years before the fall of Alamut to the Mongols. The following poems are translated from the *Kitab al-manaqib* (Karachi, 1986), and Jamal al-Din Abu'l-Qasim 'Abd Allah b. 'Ali Kashani, *Zubdat al-tawarikh: bakhsh-i Fatimiyan va Nizariyan*, ed. M.T. Danishpazhuh (2nd ed. Tehran, 1987).

THE MASTER OF THE TIME

The master of the time
is he in whose presence
the higher world bends
its back every moment
in supplication.

The dust of his footprint
is the antimony[64]
to remove the veil
that conceals the eye
of the intellect.

O master of the time!
without your consent,
it is not possible for
the world to obtain its
needs by any other means.

If you cast the shadow
of your displeasure upon
an angel, he will turn
quickly into a devil
and all his work to dust.

But if you look upon
the devil with a glance
of your favour, he will
turn into an angel, a mine
of purity and veracity.

This world, a prison
for your servants,
is suddenly transformed by
your grace and mercy into
the house of everlasting life.

Ra'is Hasan

THE HEART THAT KNOWS

The heart that knows the Imam's pleasure, receives
without a shadow of doubt the divine command.

He may appear a servant, but in essence and honour,
he rules over the inhabitants of the spiritual world.

The Holy Spirit empowers him to reach a place where
the dust under his mount turns into the philosopher's stone.

His noble soul, ascending through grades of meaning,
rises far above the flirtations of sensory distractions.

The light of his heart, by marvels and miracles,
becomes like the sun at the zenith of its splendour.

And for those who help the faith and the mission
of the Imam, he becomes their absolute master and guide.

THE CALL OF THE SPIRIT

O Hasan! Beware that from
    desire and avarice, your heart
and soul should turn into
    a quiver for arrows of lust.

Or that your high ambition,
    out of greed or desperate need
should yearn for this house
    of hypocrisy and destruction!

Know that your love of status
    is a great temptation,
for he who suffers from it
    becomes a devil himself.

The desire for wealth is
    like an ant: do not cherish it!
The ant becomes a serpent
    and the serpent a dragon.

By the grace of Almighty God,
    the time has come for you
to detach your heart from
    the creatures of this world.

Then only will you become
    one of the Qa'im's community,[65]
and have the honour of being
    a disciple of the friends of God.

Then only will come to you
    the spiritual illumination
of the true lord to grant you
    the bliss that is boundless.

GOOD FORTUNE

O brothers! When the blessed time
    comes and the good fortune of
both the worlds accompanies us,
    the king who possesses more than
a hundred thousand horsemen will
    be frightened of a single warrior.
But it is also possible that when

our good fortune is on the wane,
our spring will turn into autumn
and the autumn into spring!
Did you not see the sun of
    the great resurrection arise today
from the mountains which are the preachings
of Mustansir and the prayers of Nizar?[66]

THE RISING OF THE SUN

Glorious it arose, the bright sun
    of *'Ala dhikrihis-salam,*[67]
from the east of the threshold
    of *'Ala dhikrihis-salam.*

The promised day of "the earth will
    shine with the glory of its Lord"[68]
has appeared from the shining light
    of *'Ala dhikrihis-salam.*

All the demons of the time
    have been reduced to dust by
the powerful shooting flames
    of *'Ala dhikrihis-salam.*

The world is delivered from
    the ravages of famine through
the blessings of the open door
    of *'Ala dhikrihis-salam.*

If you have the desire to see
    at once the Tablet of the Throne,[69]
go take a look at the book
    of *'Ala dhikrihis-salam.*

Thanks be to God that he has
　　　　　become the *khalifa* to
protect and preserve the community
　　　　　of *'Ala dhikrihis-salam.*

The sword of the Qa'im has
　　　　　become unsheathed today
in the words and discourses
　　　　　of *'Ala dhikrihis-salam.*

The rain of eternal life is
　　　　　confined only to one cloud,
borne by the merciful breeze
　　　　　of *'Ala dhikrihis-salam.*

Behold now, how both cloud
　　　　　and life have come together
in the most felicitous season
　　　　　of *'Ala dhikrihis-salam.*

O Hasan! Return from the end
　　　　　to your beginning, and say:
Glorious it arose, the bright sun
　　　　　of *'Ala dhikrihis-salam.*

Nizari Quhistani

Hakim Sa'd al-Din Nizari Quhistani was an important Persian Ismaili poet who was born in Birjand, Quhistan, in 645/1247-48. His father lost all his property in the Mongol invasions when Nizari was still a child. After completing his early education, Nizari studied philosophy and literature and thereafter served as a financial administrator for the local Kart ruling dynasty based in Harat, western Afghanistan. Nizari travelled widely in the course of his career. On one of his journeys, which took him to the Caspian and Transcaucasian regions, he had an audience with the Ismaili Imam Shams al-Din Muhammad (d. c. 710/1310). A few years after his return from this journey, Nizari's court career ended abruptly as a result of political intrigues by his enemies. He was dismissed from government service, his property was confiscated, and he was exiled to his native Quhistan where he took up farming and died in 720/1320. Nizari was an accomplished poet who composed in the style of Sufi poets, and it is reported that he was personally acquainted with the poets Sa'di and Mahmud-i Shabistari. The selection of Nizari's poems is from his *Diwan*, ed. Muzahir Musaffa (Tehran, 1992).

ALEXANDER'S QUEST

When Alexander became renowned
        for his pomp and naiveté,
he went to the east while his
        object was hidden in the west.[70]

The fountain of the water of life
        did not come close to him,
because he was in the stage
        of ignorance and darkness.

His Aristotle was unaware
        of the secret of that fountain,
and its symbol was hidden
        from the precepts of the Greek.

Had it been so easy to reach
        that famous fountainhead,
Moses would not have returned
        from Khidr in bewilderment.[71]

Think of yourself as Alexander:
        what is it that you seek?
Tell me, what do you mean by
        this water and that fountain?

What do you know of the fountain
        except that it has a name?
And what is Khidr to you
        other than an imaginary being?

Nizari Quhistani

THE VIRTUE OF MA'RIFA

Do you know why the six directions are narrow for your soul?
Because you are confined within the four walls of matter.

As long as you stop at the outer meaning of the Qur'an,
you are in the twilight until you discover its inner meaning.

If you are given a tonic from the pharmacy of Oneness,
you will be cured, otherwise you will remain in your sickness.

Why do you say "heretic" to one who has established his faith
with a hundred proofs from the Qur'an and the Hadith?

When you understand he who attains the perfect *ma'rifa*,[72]
then by knowing him, you will confess your own ignorance.

You will write the document of submission with freedom,
and, like Salman, read the secret symbols of the holy Prophet.[73]

If you follow the book of God and the progeny of Muhammad,
you will be saved, otherwise you are drowned in a whirlpool.

O Nizari! You have forgotten the secret of the "deaf and dumb",[74]
otherwise you would not read such discourses to one born blind.

How is it possible to open an oyster before the blind,
as if you are offering saffron with hay to a herd of cows?

ABODE OF THE BELOVED

My beloved is not a bird
    contained in every roost and nest,
nor is he contained by
    the earth or the heaven.

He does not appear to
    reasoning or reflection,
nor is he contained in
    any location or direction.

He cannot be estimated
    nor imagined by the mind;
indeed, he cannot be contained
    anywhere in the universe.

It's imagination to try
    to sense him by ear or eye;
it's absurd to say that he
    is contained by word or speech.

His essence is not divided,
    nor is his face reflected;
neither his name nor attributes
    can be contained in the tongue.

If you have understood this much,
    you will come to understand that
he can be contained within
    the intellect and the senses.

And if you have the vision,
    you will be able to see that
he can be contained within
    the body and soul of man.

By his knowledge you will learn
  and by his light you will see;
otherwise how can knowledge
  and sight be contained in him?

I know that there's a veil
  between one soul and another;
otherwise how can he be contained
  at once in this and that?

O Nizari! How long will you
  indulge in your flights of fancy?
By God! Both the worlds are contained
  in a single particle of him!

I FOUND THE TREASURE

At the beginning, when I emerged from non-existence to existence,
  I found a hundred different defects in my life.

It was during this perplexity, when I looked at myself, that I found
  the casket containing the hidden treasure.

When I looked carefully at the court of the king of heart, I found
  the intellect as deputy and the soul as gate-keeper.

I wandered much like Alexander in search of the water of life;
  I found it because my fellow-traveller happened to be Khidr.[75]

Finally, the Noah of the time led me to the ark of guidance and
  I found myself saved from the billowing deluge.

When I firmly held the rope of God with willing submission,[76]
  I found deliverance from the pit of disappointment.

Those who search without a guide, in conformity and polytheism,
   I found them lifeless like pictures on a wall of stone.

Without the custodian and confidant of secret wisdom, I found
   the intellect perplexed in the sea of imagination.

That which mountains, oceans, earth and heaven were unable
   to bear, I found in the interior of the human body.[77]

Where once my life was feeble, barren and perplexed, I found
   every particle burning bright like the sun.

On the ladders, Gabriel let me pass step by step, until I found
   proof to the stations of the friend of God.

Alas! Who would believe me if I said that last night I found
   myself sitting with the king, knee to knee?

Now when I travel again within myself, I tell myself: "Yes, I
   found this station because of the king."

Had it been due to merit, we would be a world apart, but I have
   found the path to sit on his threshold.

Whom will I tell what my eyes have seen with certainty, that what
   cannot be found here, I found it there fully-formed?

If you trust me, then do not trust yourself, because I too
   found this treasure hidden from me at the beginning.

I do not have any capital to meet the expenses of paradise,
   although I found his favours beyond the bounds of possibility.

If you are happy with the truth, then paradise is with you;
   because from you to paradise, I have found an easy way.

He for whom the sphere has rotated from the beginning of
   existence, I found when I turned away from myself.

All things that exist end in their origination; it is only
   the ocean of love which I found boundless and fathomless.

Salvation is in the Imam of the time; I found the root
   of faith in obedience to his commands and prohibitions.

I gave up everything except "offspring, one from the other"[78]
   when I found the permanent Imamate in them.

Turn your back on the desert of time's deviations, because I
   found the path to the door of 'Ali from Salman's light.[79]

Since he raised Nizari with the hand of nurture, I found
   the foot of his esteem shining to the heights of heaven.

THE ONE ABOVE THEM ALL

It's not possible to traverse the path
of lovers with the foot of intellect,
because intellectuals are like birds
and the path of love is for them a trap.

When you have studied all the sciences,
come to me and I will show to you he
who is God's proof and witness on earth,
and the perfector of the imperfect.

Whenever you see anyone stand before you
wearing a turban, you stand behind him,
as if he is your imam – not for a breath
is the world without the Imam of the time!

If you do not know the Imam of the time
with certitude, then know for sure that
your wife, your wealth and even the head
upon your shoulders are unlawful to you.

I will sell your imam for the sweetmeats
of drunkards who have drained their cups,
because the turban that sits on his head
is worth only a pledge for wine and goblet.

And if you are a follower of two imams,
how would you answer me if I were to ask
you this question: who between them is
your real Imam, the one above them all?

It does not worry me if all the mullahs
of the world declared in their edicts
that among the chosen and the common,
the drunken Nizari is worst of them all.

I have no fear of being killed by them,
nor of the vexations of burning flesh;
I care not what wounds they inflict on me,
because they are all liars and hypocrites!

'Abd Allah Ansari

Very little is known about Khwaja 'Abd Allah Ansari, who died in the second half of the ninth/fifteenth century and should not be confused with the famous Sufi poet of the same name. He was a contemporary of the Ismaili Imam Mustansir bi'llah III, also called Gharib Mirza (d. c. 904/1498). There are some references to him in Ismaili sources of the time which indicate that 'Abd Allah was well-known for his poetic writings. Although much of his poetry has disappeared, it represents the earliest evidence of the revival of Ismaili literature in Persia in the aftermath of the Mongol invasions of Iran in the mid-seventh/thirteenth century. The following poems are from a manuscript in the library of the Institute of Ismaili Studies, London.

FORM AND ESSENCE

How strange! Each time he
    appears in a different form:
sometimes he is Mustansir
    and sometimes Salam Allah![80]

Sometimes he is a child
    and sometimes an old man;
sometimes he ascends to heaven
    or descends into a well.

Even if he has a hundred forms,
    why should the wise worry?
He whose inner eye has opened,
    is guided to him aright.

Certainly, he who does not
    follow your guidance,
though he be a dignitary
    of the court, goes astray.

By Almighty God! Whoever is
    disobedient to your command,
even an elder of the court,
    becomes a child on the path!

'Abd Allah Ansari

THE FELICITY OF GRACE

O my Mawla, you know that
in this contemptible world,
life elapses in negligence as
the months and years pass away.[81]

O my Mawla, we have not sown
a single grain in this world
for the sake of the next world,
even as time keeps slipping by.

Then an oracle invisible said
to the ear of my soul:
"Do not fear, for you have
received an unexpected felicity."

Even though I am devoid
of obedience, I am happy that
whoever becomes a *darwish* of your
court becomes a man exalted.

O my Mawla, even if I am
guilty of gross audacity,
I will not worry because your
grace accompanies me always.

Khayrkhwah-i Harati

Muhammad Rida b. Sultan Husayn, known as Khayrkhwah-i Harati, was born towards the end of the ninth/fifteenth century near Harat in western Afghanistan, and received his early education in the Persian town of Mashhad. When he was nineteen years old, his father was murdered by brigands while on his way to Anjudan for an audience with the Imam of the time, Mustansir bi'llah III. Evidently the Imam intended to appoint Khayrkhwah's father as the chief *da'i* of the Khurasan, Badakshan and Kabul areas, but soon after his father's death, Khayrkhwah was himself taken to Anjudan and subsequently appointed *da'i* in his father's place. Thereafter, he devoted himself to the Ismaili cause for the rest of his life. Khayrkhwah was a prolific writer and poet who used the pen-name of "Gharibi" in his verses. He died sometime after 960/1553. His poems are selected from W. Ivanow's edition of *Tasnifat-i Khayrkhwah-i Harati* (Tehran, 1961).

THE MIRACLE OF KNOWLEDGE

The sign and miracle
of our master came
from the beginning
of the command "Be!"[82]

According to
the common folk,
these are clear in his
designation and lineage.

But according to
the chosen ones,
it is other than this.
Do you know what it is?

It is the miracle
of his knowledge,
revealed only to
the eye of the intellect.

Khayrkhwah-i Harati

THE THREE WORLDS

Why does the manifestation
of the divine command dwell
in this place, this half-way
station-house of travellers?

Because it is his desire that
the three worlds should not perish,
and other than him no one can
be perfect in the three worlds.[83]

His existence with the people
of unity is in a spiritual way,
known only to those like Salman,
of whom was said "He is from me."[84]

With the people of gradation,
he manifests himself with
a special kind of teaching,
as the Imam of the righteous.

For the people of opposition,
he is with them through his
intellect and reasoning,
as a true and real witness.

But if you are not to become
one of the polytheists, know
that his manifestations are
only relative, not absolute.

Thus you will recognize
the master of the three worlds;
then know also his proof, Gharibi,
who has recognized the truth.

Khaki Khurasani

The details of Imam Quli Khaki Khurasani's life are not known, but it can be deduced from his poetry that he lived in the eleventh/ seventeenth century during the time of two Ismaili Imams, Dhu'l-Faqar 'Ali (d. 1043/1634) and Nur al-Din (d. 1082/1671). He was born into a land-owning family of Dizbad, a village in the mountains between Mashhad and Nishapur in northern Khurasan. Khaki appears to have spent most of his life there as a farmer, an occupation which he combined with the composition of poetry. It was probably on account of his open espousal of the Ismaili cause in his poetry that he was persecuted and tortured. However, this experience does not seem to have dented his enthusiasm for his faith or love for poetry, which he continued to compose until his death sometimes after 1056/1646. The poems are selected from *An Abbreviated Version of the Diwan of Khaki Khurasani*, ed. W. Ivanow (Bombay, 1933).

THE INNER REALITY

The love of Mawla
affects my heart in a way known
only to the one who
is aware of it.

The inner reality
of the 'Ali of the time is not
the same as his
outward forms.

He is the manifestation
of every wonder in the world,
his state different
at every time.

Sometimes visible,
and sometimes concealed from us,
he travels between being
and non-being.

His reality is
the fruit of the goodly tree
which is mentioned
in the Qur'an.[85]

The allusion to
"offspring, one from the other"[86]
means that after the father
comes the son.

One entrusts
the essence to the other when
the body and the name
have to change.

Khaki Khurasani

Everyone's profit
is derived from his intellect;
Khaki's loss comes from
his carnal soul!

ANCHOR OF THE SHIP

The secret of the chosen is
                    revealed to the ecstatic;
the ordinary ascetic knows
                    only how to stammer.

The lord in this world
                    is the anchor of the ship;
the lord of religion is the pearl
                    in the ocean of meanings.

Know for certain that what
                    I tell you is the truth;
alas, those who are stupid
                    do not believe in it.

The light of Muhammad and
                    'Ali is one and the same,[87]
but those who are in pursuit
                    of falsehood know this not.

I am Khaki, the faithful
                    dog of Mawla's religion,
whereas the dogs of the world
                    bark only for a carcass.

Shaykh Khudr

Not much is known about al-Hajj Shaykh Khudr, who was a contemporary of the Ismaili Imam Nizar II (d. 1134/1722). He was born in Qadmus, Syria, and in his adult life is known to have visited Persia for an audience with the Imam who appointed him to a senior position in the Syrian Ismaili community. Shaykh Khudr lived for approximately seventy years and was buried in Khirbat al-Faras in Khawabi in central Syria. The following selection of his poems are translated from *al-Anashid al-diniyya* (Salamiyya, Syria, 1973).

SHIPS OF SALVATION

The people of
the house of Prophethood
are the manifestations of light.

They are that
which exists forever
and in what has already elapsed.

They are the ships
of salvation for those
who come running to them with hope.[88]

They are the rain
abundant in moisture,
and their grace is the best of springs.

The essence of
their souls is knowledge
from a world beyond the intellects.

Indeed, it is
their invitation which
rescues souls from the pit of destruction.

Shaykh Khudr

THE AWE-INSPIRING LIGHT

O Lord of creatures, from You
radiated the awe-inspiring light,
illuminating the world so that
what is hidden becomes manifest.

The absolute real essence is
the light of an everlasting sun,
incandescent from the flames
of its hidden meanings.

How many times has it appeared
from the veils of the beginning?
It is nothing less than our
refuge on the Day of Summons.

It looks upon the two worlds
in the springs of eternity,
and from it descends the spirit
of command and the reward.

There is a secret inviolable
in the manifestation of this
light by which souls are guided
to their origin and source.

He is the holy of holies,
from whom knowledge is acquired,
the mine whose precious gems will
be revealed on the Day of Reckoning.

THE TRUSTWORTHY SPIRIT

When the morning breeze
    blew in the tree of birds,
the celestial circling
    sphere was delighted.

And the trustworthy spirit,
    the custodian of light,
descended with his
    unique revelation.[89]

The minarets rose high
    and guidance became clear,
when the custodian of cycles
    manifested himself.

Our souls glanced at him
    when he inclined his head,
a sovereign most noble
    and magnificent to look at.

His face shining bright with
    sublime intimations,
his will a revered light
    and a double-edged sword!

Shaykh Khudr

THE COMING OF YOUR LIGHT

O heavenly bird!
   O you whose mission is
the service of God,
   unique in every way!

You are the origin
   of the appearance
of our lords, one from
   another, in every age.

As torrential rain
   brings nourishing water,
you bring to the soul
   news of the unseen.

Through you the days
   have reached the limit
of their perfection,
   and the nights are erased.

Man never understood
   the meaning of his soul,
until he observed
   the coming of your light.

CUPBEARER OF THE NIGHT

The luminous full-moon
is the night's cupbearer;
at his coming, the darkness
vanishes like a fugitive slave.

Familiarity can find
nothing but kindness from
him, as if his sanctuary
were the icon of a monk.

Short in stature and
hidden in substance,
he aspires to the human
with the passion of desire.

He crosses the gardens
crowned with contentment,
like a star by the side
of a planet as it sets.

An outcry of the stars
trembles in him from
around the circumference
of the sphere that surrounds him.

And the trustworthy spirit
descends among the worlds
with the determination
of a brilliant shooting star.

Shaykh Khudr

LOVE IN SECLUSION

O people of the house of God
    that endures in the heavenly world:
        indeed you are my desire and purpose.

Your beauty is the target of my eyes,
    your secret is the treasure of my heart,
        and your light is my observation post.

I swear by the seclusions I spend
    in your love, and I cry out for you
        in the early hours of the morning.

My eyes yearn only for your beauty,
    and all day long, my heart does not
        remember anything other than you.

IN THE COURTYARD OF LOVE

How wonderful
is the success of those
who reach the abode of peace
and gain the object of their desire!

Delighted by
his noble presence,
their souls are transformed by
his honour and glory as they meet him.

They dismount
to receive from him
the abundance of his mercy,
and prostrate themselves before him.

Now they look
at his beauty with
the inner eye of their hearts,
as they dance in joy to welcome him.

They attained
to their soul's desire
because of their obedience to
the knowledge of the truth among them.

In the divine
courtyard of love,
generosity has lifted the veil
and put the demons of darkness to flight!

Shaykh Khudr

THE FRUITS OF REALITY

The pitch-dark night
  is perishing;
the beloved is in the Pleiades;[90]
  the cupbearer
of wine draws near to me.

A subtle spiritual form
  becomes manifest,
whose abode is Mars, bearing
  in his hands
a shattering sword.

And when he appeared
  in the darkness
of your troubled heart, you saw
  a brilliant light
shining forth from it.

How pleasant are the fruits
  of reality!
In their subtle meanings
  is a harvest
for every reaper of fruits!

THE CALL OF THE FRIEND

The cooing of the dove delighted the trees
because of a meeting he has with the friend:
it is a high and glorious destination,
    which is our eternal source,
    which is our eternal source...

There is a King above the heavens who
excels others by the intensity of His light,
and the soul is driven to Him
    when the friend calls to it,
    when the friend calls to it.

When it is called, the soul at once speeds
to him and receives the guidance it needs,
and the rust is removed from it
    by the physician's remedy,
    by the physician's remedy.

And as the soul is filled with brilliance,
all the pain and suffering vanish from it,
until it attains what it desires
    with the universal Good
    with the universal Good.

This is the soul's supreme achievement,
at the time of return, which it has sought
ever since it first heard the call of
    the friend of the Knower,
    the friend of the Knower.

Whoever comes to this blessed place
and reaches the threshold of the Imam's door,
his desire is fulfilled and he alights
    in the abode of paradise,
    in the abode of paradise.

Shaykh Khudr

Then he goes around the world in the form
of a hidden light and becomes a noble mountain
of honour, to whom Moses comes close,
    he who conversed with God,
    he who conversed with God.

At the break of dawn he appears as a bright
pulsating star giving out flashes of light,
a soul arisen in the east with
    a clear and melodious voice,
    a clear and melodious voice.

And from the edge of the western horizon
comes an angel who whispers to his heart
the secret meaning of the sunset,
    and brings the dead to life,
    and brings the dead to life.

Our resolve will never cease in its devotion
to the descendants of the Prophet –
that is the Ka'ba where we alight,
    the heart's sacred sanctuary,
    the heart's sacred sanctuary.

There is a fine translucent veil in them,
through which shines a most affable spirit,
and the secret of an ineffable mystery,
    received from the Lord,
    received from the Lord.

THE CITY OF SHINING LIGHT

There is a city ruled by the king of kings,
to whom surrendered the necks of infidel kings,
a city in which the light of Imamate shines forth,
and a spirit from the angelic world dwells.

It is a city to which God sent His guidance,
establishing in it the proof of His authority,[91]
a city that radiates all around it a glow
of light coming from a far distant past.

O glorious city in whose garden there is
the seed of paradise and the ripening of fruits!
O blessed guarded city whose manifold meanings
are hidden from the eyes of the spectators!

The cities under his shadow and flag are like
the sun and the moon in the heavens above;
the time of the world is ordered within them,
and the light which they emit dazzles the eye.

There is a city fixed from eternity for
the son of the Imam, the chosen, the valiant;
it is the loftiest of cities in the creation;
it is an invitation to the Oneness of God.

Fida'i Khurasani

"Fida'i" was the pen-name of Muhammad b. Zayn al-'Abidin Khurasani, a descendant of the poet Khaki Khurasani of Dizbad. He was born in the same village in northern Khurasan around 1266/ 1850. After completing his early education, Fida'i went to Mashhad for higher studies, which included theology and jurisprudence. As the most learned of the Khurasani Ismailis, he travelled to India several times to meet the 48th Ismaili Imam, Sultan Muhammad Shah, Aga Khan III (d. 1376/1957), who appointed him as *mu'allim*, the chief religious instructor of his community in Iran. Besides being a prolific poet, Fida'i was the author of several works on Ismaili theology, law and history. He died in 1342/1923 and was buried next to the grave of Khaki Khurasani in Dizbad. The poems are from his *Mathnawi-i nigaristan*, also known as *Qasida-i nigaristan*, ed. A.A. Semenov, in *Iran*, 3 (1929).

THE WEALTH OF THIS WORLD

All the wealth and feeding of this world is like mud;
what can you obtain from mud except affliction?

Your heart has become a slave to the wealth of this world;
listen, how can you ever become the slave of God?

Since you are a seeker of office, wealth and honour,
you do not know that each of them is a pit for you.

You are like a greedy ant, ever gathering and hoarding;
how can you incline towards attaining perfection?

You toil and struggle so much for the sake of this world,
that even the devils are ashamed of what you do.

By 'Ali's love, let your heart be cleansed and purified.
Make the dust of his path collyrium for your eyes.[92]

REMEMBRANCE OF THE HEART

O heart, come and listen
    to the attributes of Haydar,[93]
so that by praising him,
    you become bright as the moon.

Know that he whose nature
    is pure and sincere seeks
the remembrance of the Imam
    with all his heart and soul.

He who does not seek
    the Imam's remembrance is
devoid of wisdom and his heart
    is plunged in darkness.

But he who praises him
    from the depths of his soul,
his heart becomes illumined
    by the light of faith.

He who seeks to praise 'Ali
    acquires the secrets of faith,
and his heart becomes filled
    with sublime knowledge.

Truly, he who seeks the Imam
    in the remembrance of him,
the light in his heart burns
    brighter than the moon.

RECOGNITION OF THE IMAM

He is always present,
    a witness with his followers;
but who has seen his beauty
    except the blessed?

He who is the cupbearer of
    the fount of paradise,
is aware altogether of
    the hearts of his followers.

He is the Imam of the time,
    the guide and comforter,
the protector of his followers,
    whether young or old.

Like the sun in the sky,
    he is manifest in the world,
but the blind bat cannot see
    his luminous face.

Why are you always in doubt
    and suspicion like Satan?
Do not forget to remember 'Ali
    even for a single moment.

If you do not see 'Ali
    in this world, know that on
the Day of Judgement, you will
    be resurrected blind.

Like a bird enticed by grain,
    you are entangled in a trap;
therefore you do not see
    the Solomon of your time.

If you fail to recognize
    the Imam of the time, you will
take nothing to your grave
    but sighs and remorse.

If you will not take to
    your heart the love of Haydar,
there will be nothing for you
    but sorrow and regret.

If you do not let the love
    of Mawla enter your soul,
you will become like a renegade
    and die like an infidel.

IF YOU HAVE MAWLA'S LOVE

If you have Mawla's love, you are an excellent man,
otherwise be sure that you are less than a devil.

If you have Mawla's love in your heart, you are a king,
otherwise be sure that you are less than a straw.

If you have Mawla's love in the heart, you are a light,
otherwise be sure that you are less than an ant.

If you have Mawla's love in your heart, you are rich,
otherwise be sure that you are less than a beggar.

If you have Mawla's love, you are truly a noble man,
otherwise be sure that you are less than a shepherd.

If you have Mawla's love in your heart, you are a soul,
otherwise be sure that there is no real life in you.

Except for 'Ali's friendship, nothing is profitable to you,
except for 'Ali's love, you are neither alive nor dead.

'Allama Nasir Hunzai

'Allama Nasir al-Din Hunzai was born in 1335/1917 in Hydarabad, a
town in Hunza, which is situated in the northern areas of Pakistan. In
addition to his poetry in Persian, Turkish and Urdu, he is the first
poet to compose in his native language of Burushaski, on account of
which he is known as "Baba-i Burushaski". 'Allama Nasir has also
written several works on aspects of the Ismaili faith. The poems trans-
lated here are from his *Jawahir-i haqa'iq* (Karachi, 1975), *Bihishte
Asquring* (Karachi, 1988) and *Jawahir-i ma'arif* (Karachi, n.d.).

THE SLAVE OF MAWLA ʿALI

I am the slave of Mawla ʿAli,
    of Shah Sultan who is my ʿAli;
my obedience, pilgrimage and prayer,
    my religion and faith is ʿAli.

When I heard of God's hidden
    treasure and searched for it,
I did not find any except ʿAli;
    my secret treasure is ʿAli.

I do not weep from pain and grief,
    but for the sake of his vision;
my comfort, light and healing;
    my refuge and remedy is ʿAli.

By the grace of Mawla ʿAli,
    all my purposes are achieved;
my soul's refuge, my kind lord,
    my help and saviour is ʿAli.

The lion in the enemy's ranks,
    the conqueror of Khaybar is ʿAli,[94]
the sovereign of the time and
    the lord of the valiant is ʿAli.

There's no sword like Dhu'l-faqar;[95]
    and no ideal man like ʿAli;
you are my helper in every
    calamity, O my protector ʿAli.

The allusion to "rope of God"[96]
    is to the firm handle of ʿAli;
the owner and guardian of paradise
    is none other than ʿAli.

Know that the 'Ali of our time
  is Sultan Muhammad Shah, who
is generous in both the worlds,
  and the king of all kings.[97]

QUATRAINS OF LOVE

Until I gain the friendship of
my sovereign of both the worlds,
I will continue to roast my
liver in the fire of his love.

> My beloved does not appear
> to the world-seeing eye until
> the antimony of devotion
> illumines the eye of the intellect.

If the tree of my life does not
bear the fruit of your love,
then let the saw of death cut it
down from the top to its roots.

> I make incense of your love
> by casting the wild rue of my soul
> into the fire; but alas, you show
> no mercy even as I burn.

When my pen cries, unable
to describe your pure attributes,
then I too shed tears until my
entire skirt is drenched in blood.

> The journey of pure love to
> the destination of his vision
> is difficult; courage therefore,
> until you traverse the carnal soul!

Shimmering Light

I will await you continually,
even though my sight fades away,
until the miraculous light of
your footsteps draws near to me.

> The festival of spiritual bliss
> does not arrive until
> the crescent of the moon appears
> in the firmament of vision.

O my soul! I never suffered
from the wounds of love until that
fateful day when the arrowhead
of your glance transfixed my heart.

> I have dedicated my life entirely
> to the cause of his love; now
> I will sit in his remembrance
> until my body ceases to be.

O seeker! Now that you have come
underneath the tree of wisdom,
be patient until the fruit
of intellect falls to you by itself.

> What a wonderful stream poured
> from my eyes in the springtime
> of spiritual light until my heart
> began to blossom from end to end!

I had neither knowledge nor
the strength to acquire it until
you, the living book of light, began
to speak in my heart with wisdom.

> Many a night have I spent in
> the remembrance of your name
> and intoxication of your love,
> until the light of dawn burst out.

The auspicious outpouring of
sparks from my voice does not come
until the glowing embers of his love
are cast in the veils of my heart.

> The lord of the beloved
> has already left, even before
> we had a glimpse of him to
> the satisfaction of our hearts.

It is not easy for me to hold
his hem, for even as I extend
my hand, he turns away with
a flourish of his luminescent skirt!

> O friends, divulge not to people
> the secret of his beauty until
> they have lost the desire for
> the mad scramble of this world!

When the frenzied Nasir comes,
he throws up flames of yearning,
until the fire flares up in
the happy assembly of friends.

THE TREASURE OF LUQMAN

Thousands of rubies and gems
    are locked in the rock of the self;
O ignorant one, do not delay
    in digging them out yourself!

If you want to taste the fruit of
    the tree of eminence, try to
first sow the seed of your ego
    in the soil of humility.

The light of a flame does not
    welcome moist wood because of
its pride in the darkness and
    deception of self-conceit.

Enrich yourself with qualities
    of faith and wisdom, since it is
in poverty that you will find
    the hidden treasure of Luqman.[98]

The rich have a dire need for
    the firm prop of religion;
otherwise they tumble down
    intoxicated by their wealth.

GLAD TIDINGS FOR THE SOUL

May hundreds of glad tidings be to the soul,
for the Imam of the time has arrived;
the bearer of the manifested light,
and the divine splendour has arrived.

As with the Prophet, there are legions
of angels before him and after him;
like the noble Abu'l-Hasan, with
honour and elegance, he has arrived.[99]

The casket of pearls is created
from the five treasures of religion,[100]
but all the virtues of those five are
encompassed in him who has arrived.

His breath fills the garden of existence
with colour and fragrance most sublime;
as the season of new spring arrives
to the meadows, he has arrived.

The dwelling-place of the beloved
is truly in the hearts of his lovers;
congratulations to you, O heart, because
to his abode my lord has arrived.

Intoxicated by the sweet fragrance
of the beloved, my soul declared:
"The giver of essence to the navel
of Tartary's musk-deer has arrived."

The star by whose influence the stone
is transformed into ruby, and the heaven
which has caused the pearl of Eden
to come into existence, has arrived.

It is in order to instruct the souls
in the school of the realities of faith
that the master who has the knowledge
of everything, open and hidden, has arrived.

For the sake of your body and soul,
sometimes appearing in physical form
and sometimes in spirit, sometimes in public
and sometimes in secret, he has arrived.

The sun which arises with the light
of his beauty and casts the radiance
of his countenance upon the souls of
all his lovers near and far, has arrived.

Fall not in love with the shoots that
ever sprout in the garden of this world,
for he who grows cypress and jasmine
in the garden of the spirit has arrived.

In the banquet of secret knowledge
for the souls of lovers, the fragrance
of "I breathed into him My spirit"[101]
from the beloved's lips has arrived.

He who is the all-embracing intellect,
the benefactor of both the material
and the spiritual worlds, the master
of every knowledge and skill, has arrived.

Before you came, the bird of my soul
had flown away from the body's cage,
but it has now returned to its home
since into my body you have arrived.

Upon the dust of your path I sacrifice
the drop of my soul because to this
assembly of lovers the ocean of
the all-inclusive soul has arrived.

The colour and countenance of lovers
have blossomed like a rose in springtime,
for the giver of colour to the rosy-cheeked
cornelian of Yemen has arrived.[102]

The affectionate spiritual physician
has cured me without becoming apparent,
since the redeemer of every affliction
by means of his affection has arrived.

The troublesome thoughts that once did
plague my heart have gone forever,
because he who is the soul of peace,
repose and security has arrived.

O brothers! Abandon your love of
the idol-temple of existence, because
the light of the Creator of every
beauty in the world has arrived.

O Nasir! Convey his beauty and grace
to the eyes and ears of lovers, and may
hundreds of glad tidings be to the soul,
for the Imam of the time has arrived.

SECRETS OF THE HEART

Only miracles are there in light,
    only the secret of the Compassionate;
I have learnt from the custodian of light
    the secret of the wise Qur'an.

In the palace of light are secrets
    known only to the chosen ones;
what can a beggar in the street know of
    the secret of the king of miracles?

Even though earthlings fly on high
    to the moon on the wings of science,
they know not the secret of
    the beloved who dwells in my heart.

O friends! Do not reveal to others
    the miracle of love's consummation,
for how can they ever comprehend
    the secret of Solomon's throne?

Keep the secret treasure of 'Ali's
    love and eminence in your heart;
why divulge in vain the secret of he
    who is the king of the valiant?

The man who knows the eternal light
    is a secret known only to God,
but He who is the exalted lord
    is a secret known to man.

If you know the key to the Qur'an,
    you can enter the treasure-house of light;
the Imam is the lord of the command,
    thus await the secret of his command.

Open your inner eye and see
    the splendour of the scene of light;
read in the book of unveiling
    about the secret of 'Ali's glory.

O beloved! No one knows the word
    of my love's pleasure other than you;
only you know the secret of
    the yearning that sways my heart.

Follow the guidance of the light
    because the lamp is lit and manifest;
understand from the verse of light[103]
    the source of the secret of faith.

Become an angel of the time
    and bow yourself before Adam if you
are able to understand the secret
    of the image of the merciful.

Our Nasir has now succeeded
    in the recognition of unity;
know that he found the secret of
    that recognition in the wine of love.

Isma'il Adra

Born in 1927, Isma'il Adra received his early education at Salamiyya, Syria, before proceeding to study Arabic language and literature at Damascus University and embarking on a life-long career in teaching. He started writing poetry in his youth and several of his poems have appeared in Arabic journals and newspapers. He also wrote short stories and articles on Muslim philosophy and Ismailism. Isma'il Adra died in 1981 and a collection of his poems is to be published shortly. The following verses are from *al-Anashid al-diniyya* (Salamiyya, Syria, 1973).

A NOBLE BIRTHDAY

The Imam is born...
 O heavens, rejoice!
 O earth, bedeck
  yourself and sing!

Today is the *'id*...
 O daisies, open!
  Diffuse your sweet
   fragrance and celebrate!

The clouds disperse...
 O sun, irradiate!
  Unveil your beauty
   and spread it abroad!

The sky is clear...
 O lovers, come!
  Prepare a feast for
   his noble birthday!

Isma'il Adra

MY BREATHLESS HEART

O Karim! O my sovereign![104]
    You are my destination
and to you I come running
    with a breathless heart.

Come close to me in
    your love and presence,
with that which is between
    your purity and mercy.

Since I have made you
    the sovereign of my heart,
increase its yearning for you
    who are so near to me.

Grant me your pleasure
    that I live in its gardens,
and return to me when
    you reject my patience.

Since to refrain from
    you and your love is
prohibited, O my sovereign,
    let me melt in your love.

And make my lot your
    pleasant neighbourhood
on the day we meet in
    the rose-garden of eternity.

I have none other than you,
    so torment not a lover
who comes running to you
    with a breathless heart.

Notes

1. Reference to the Qur'an 27:8: "And when he (Moses) came to it (the fire), he heard a voice: 'Blessed are those in the fire and those around it, and glory be to God, the Lord of the worlds.'"

2. The "children of Fatima" are the Shi'i Imams descended from the marriage of the Prophet Muhammad's daughter, Fatima, and his cousin, 'Ali ibn Abi Talib, the first Imam.

3. The terms *wali Allah* (friend of God), *khalifat Allah* (vicegerent of God) and *hujjat Allah* (proof of God), are used in Shi'i theology to designate the Prophet and the Imams. On the secondary usage of the term *hujja*, see note 39 below.

4. In this verse, the Imams are seen as custodians of the text of the revelation (*tanzil*), and as the authoritative sources of its esoteric interpretation (*ta'wil*). On *ta'wil*, see note 34 below.

5. The "progeny of Hashim" refers to the Prophet Muhammad and the Shi'i Imams as descendants of Hashim ibn 'Abd Manaf, who was the Prophet's great-grandfather.

6. 'Ad was an ancient, prosperous Arab nation mentioned in the Qur'an (26:123–140). When the people of 'Ad rejected the message of the prophet Hud, they were overwhelmed by a violent storm.

7. The sense of this verse is that the knowledge of the Imams is not dependent on divination of any kind, such as that based on omens or a person's physical features.

8. Abu Tamim Ma'add al-Mu'izz li-Din Allah (d. 365/975) was the fourth Fatimid caliph and 14th Ismaili Imam, in whose time Fatimid rule was extended across the whole of North Africa, from Ifriqiya to Egypt.

9. On "Ma'add", see note 8 above.

10. The Mother of the Book (*umm al-kitab*) is mentioned several times in the Qur'an (3:7, 13:39, 43:4) in terms of the original foundation or heavenly prototype of all revelations.

11. Reference to the Qur'an 2:37: "Then Adam received words of inspiration from his Lord, and He turned to him mercifully"; 37:146–147: "We caused a gourd plant to grow over him (Jonah) and We sent him (on a mission) to a hundred thousand (men) or more."

12. Reference to the Qur'an 26:119–120: "So We delivered him (Noah) and those with him in the laden ark, and We drowned those who remained behind."

13. On the term "proof of God", see note 3 above.

14. The Qur'an refers to 'Isa ibn Maryam, i.e. Jesus, as *al-Masih* (the Messiah, literally "the Redeemer") in 3:45 and 4:157. In this verse, it is the Imam's spiritual authority and soteriological function which is compared to that of the Messiah.

15. Ahmad, one of the noble names of the Prophet Muhammad which occurs in the Qur'an in connection with a prophecy by Jesus of an apostle to come after him (61:6).

16. Reference to the Qur'an 23:115: "Did you think that We had created you in vain?"; 75:36: "Does man think that he is to be left without an aim?"

17. Dhu'l-faqar, the name of the famous double-edged sword which the Prophet Muhammad presented to Imam 'Ali.

18. Jawhar al-Siqilli (d. 381/992) was the chief Fatimid general in the time of Imam al-Mu'izz. The poems here are from a *qasida* about the military expedition which led to the establishment of Fatimid rule over Egypt in 358/969.

19. In Muslim tradition, the *jinn* are believed to be invisible spirits which possess intelligence and are capable of doing good or evil. According to the Qur'an, they were created of smokeless fire (55:15) and the Prophet Muhammad was sent to guide them as well as mankind (46:29).

20. On the term "Hashimite", here used as a synonym for the Fatimids, see note 5 above.

21. On Imam al-Mu'izz, see note 8 above.

22. Nawruz (literally "new day"), the Persian spring festival at the vernal equinox, which is celebrated widely in Iran, Iraq, Turkey, Central and South Asia. In Shi'ism, Nawruz has acquired a special religious significance because of its association with the event of Ghadir Khumm on 18 Dhu'l-Hijja 10/632 when, according to the Shi'is, the Prophet declared Imam 'Ali as his successor.

23. Abu Mansur Nizar al-'Aziz bi'llah (d. 386/996) was the fifth Fatimid caliph and 15th Ismaili Imam, in whose period the Fatimid empire reached its farthest extent from the Atlantic in the west to Syria in the east.

24. *Haydar* (lion) is one of the names used for Imam 'Ali, on account of his exceptional courage on the battlefield which was also praised by the Prophet who called him *Asad Allah* (the lion of God).

25. Abu Tamim Ma'add al-Mustansir bi'llah (d. 487/1094) was the eighth Fatimid caliph and eighteenth Ismaili Imam. His reign of nearly sixty years, which is considered to be one of the longest in Ismaili history, marked the zenith of Fatimid power, prosperity and cultural life.

26. Thursday was an important occasion for al-Mu'ayyad, as it was on this day that he delivered his weekly "lectures of wisdom" (*majalis al-hikma*) at the Dar al-'Ilm academy in Cairo.

27. Reference to the Qur'an 37:41–49, 38:49–52, etc., for the symbolic description of the heavenly garden used by the poet.

28. On Imam al-Mustansir, see note 25 above. His father and grandfather were the Imams al-Zahir li-I'zaz Din Allah (d. 427/1036) and al-Hakim bi-Amr Allah (d. 411/1021), the seventh and sixth Fatimid caliphs respectively.

29. The quote is from the famous *hadith*: "Seek knowledge from the cradle to the grave, and seek for it even unto China."

30. *Al-Zahra* (the resplendent) is a designation used for Fatima, the Prophet's daughter and wife of Imam 'Ali. For *Haydar*, see note 24 above.

31. Hasan and Husayn were the two sons of Imam 'Ali and Fatima, and the sole grandsons of the Prophet. The poet plays upon the similarity of the Arabic letters *sin* and *shin* in their names to indicate their affinity and kinship.

32. On Dhu'l-faqar, see note 17 above.

33. A reference to the Prophetic tradition: "O 'Ali, you are to me as Aaron was to Moses, except that there will be no prophet after me."

34. *Ta'wil*, which is a Qur'anic term, literally means "to take something back to its origin". Technically, it means to understand the inner, esoteric meaning (*batin*) of a Qur'anic text, religious prescription or natural phenomenon from its outer, exoteric sense (*zahir*). The operation of *ta'wil*, which is usually distinguished from *tafsir*, the exoteric philological interpretation of the Qur'an, was practised widely among the Shi'is, particularly the Ismailis, as well as the Sufis and the philosophers. In Shi'ism, the Prophet and the Imams are the authoritative sources and dispensers of *ta'wil*.

35. The expression *ashab al-kisa'* (people of the cloak) refers to the Prophet's family and the event when the Prophet covered 'Ali, Fatima, Hasan and Husayn under his mantle, which gave rise to the following revelation of the Qur'an: "And God only wishes to remove all abominations from you, O members of the family, and to make you pure and spotless" (33:33).

36. Reference to the Qur'an 17:44: "The seven heavens and the earth and whatever is in them glorify Him; there is not a single thing but it glorifies (Him) with His praise."

37. Reference to the Qur'an 17:72: "And whoever is blind in this life will be blind in the hereafter."

38. Reference to the Qur'an 2:197: "And take provision (with you) for the journey, but verily the best provision is piety."

39. Nasir-i Khusraw used the term *hujja* (proof) as his pen-name in many

of his verses, signifying his high rank in the Fatimid *da'wa* organization. The *hujja* was responsible for the *da'wa* activities in a major region of the Muslim world, in Nasir's case Khurasan and Badakhshan. On the primary usage of the term *hujja* for the Imam, see note 3 above.

40. In Arabic, the expression "Zayd, Amr and Bakr" is used in the same idiomatic sense as "Tom, Dick and Harry" in English for ordinary persons or people taken at random.

41. *Mustafa* (the chosen) is one of the epithets used for the Prophet Muhammad.

42. "The Supreme Name" refers to one of the "beautiful names of God" (*al-asma al-husna*) given by the Prophet or the Imam of the time to their followers for the remembrance of God.

43. The master (*khwaja*) mentioned here and in the following poem is the famous Ismaili *da'i* and theologian, al-Mu'ayyad fi'l-Din al-Shirazi.

44. In the original, the poet mentions the angels Ridwan and Malik as the guardians of paradise and hell, respectively.

45. The Qur'an mentions seven gates of hell, one for each class of sinners (15:44), but does not indicate the number of gates in paradise. This was later fixed in Muslim tradition at eight owing to the greater number of souls who would benefit from God's mercy on the Last Day.

46. On *jinn*, see note 19 above.

47. Mount Qaran is in the Mazandaran province of northern Iran.

48. The "seven spheres" are the seven planetary bodies of Ptolemaic astronomy, i.e. Saturn, Jupiter, Mars, Sun, Venus, Mercury and Moon.

49. The idea of seven climes on earth between the equator and the poles is to be found in the writings of many traditional Muslim authors on geography.

50. In common with ancient and medieval European thinkers, many Muslim writers held that all creatures were constituted from a combination of the four qualitative elements, namely heat, cold, dryness and moistness, derived from the four elements of fire, air, water and earth.

51. The eighth and ninth spheres were added to the Ptolemaic system of seven spheres by Muslim astronomers to account for the heaven of the fixed stars and the outermost heaven.

52. The "ten witnesses" are the five external senses of hearing, vision, smell, taste and touch, and the five internal senses which have been variously defined by Muslim philosophers. According to Ibn Sina, these are common sense, retention of the forms and shapes of sensible objects, estimation, memory, and imagination.

53. On Nawruz, see note 22 above.

54. Capella, the name of a star of the first magnitude in the constellation Auriga.

55. The Pleiades, a cluster of stars in the constellation Taurus.

56. Darius I (522–486 BC), one of the Persian kings of the Achaemenid

dynasty, who was noted for his administrative reforms and great building projects.

57. Duldul, the name of the white mule ridden by Imam 'Ali.

58. The concepts of *zahir* (the exoteric, outward or literal meaning of revelation) and *batin* (its esoteric, inner or symbolic meaning) are fundamental principles of hermeneutic exegesis (*ta'wil*) in Shi'ism and Sufism. See note 34 above.

59. The *laylat al-qadr* (Night of Power or Honour) is the most auspicious and blessed night in the month of Ramadan, during which the Qur'an was first revealed to the Prophet Muhammad. This event is described in the Qur'an 97 and 44:3–4.

60. For an account of the rites and stations associated with the pilgrimage to Mecca, see the article "Hadjdj" in the *Encyclopaedia of Islam* (2nd ed., Leiden, 1960–), vol.3, pp. 31–8.

61. The *ashab al-kahf* (companions of the cave) refers to the story in the Qur'an (18:9–26) about a number of youths who conceal themselves in a cave to escape religious persecution.

62. The seven planets and four elements of traditional Muslim cosmology. See notes 48 and 51 above.

63. Reference to the Qur'an 17:70: "And surely We have honoured the children of Adam and conferred on them special favours above a great part of Our creation."

64. Antimony (*kuhl*), a brittle metallic element which, when calcined and powdered, is used as a cosmetic for blackening the eyelids and eyebrows.

65. The term *Qa'im* (the riser or resurrector) was used in early pre-Fatimid Ismaili thought for the eschatological Imam expected in the future. In the Ismaili teachings of the Alamut period, the term came to be applied to the Imam of the time.

66. The two Ismaili Imams mentioned here are the Fatimids al-Mustansir bi'llah (see note 25 above) and his son and designated heir, Nizar al-Mustafa li-Din Allah (d. 488/1095), who was deprived of his succession rights by the powerful *wazir* and commander of the armies, al-Afdal ibn Badr al-Jamali.

67. *'Ala-dhikrihis-salam* (he on whose mention be peace) was the honorific title of the 23rd Ismaili Imam, Hasan (d. 561/1166).

68. Reference to the Qur'an 39:69.

69. The Tablet of Throne (*lawh-i 'arsh*), a reference to *lawh al-mahfuz* (the Well-preserved Tablet) mentioned in the Qur'an (85:21–22) and identified by some Muslim commentators with the *umm al-kitab* (Mother of the Book). See note 10 above.

70. Alexander the Great (d. 324 BC), the king of Macedonia who overthrew the Persian Achaemenid empire and invaded India, was the subject of fabulous stories in Arabic and Persian literatures. One of the motifs

popular among Muslim writers was that of Alexander's vain search for the fountain of eternal life.

71. In Muslim tradition, Khidr or al-Khadir is the name given to the travelling companion and guide of Moses mentioned in the Qur'an (28: 60–82).

72. The term *ma'rifa* (sometimes translated as "gnosis") is a technical expression used primarily in Sufism for spiritual knowledge derived through an intuitive and illuminative cognition of the divine. In Ismaili thought, the term also signifies the spiritual recognition of one's own soul which is tantamount to the recognition of God.

73. Salman al-Farsi was a Persian Companion of the Prophet Muhammad, who is highly regarded in Shi'ism for his intimacy with the Prophet and his family as expressed in the Prophetic tradition "Salman is of my family", and for his defence of Imam 'Ali's right of succession to the Prophet. Salman is also venerated as one of the principal links in the chain of spiritual initiation in Sufism.

74. Reference to the Qur'an 2:18: "Deaf, dumb and blind, they will not return (to the path)."

75. See notes 70 and 71 above.

76. Reference to the Qur'an 3:103: "And hold fast all together by the rope of God and be not divided among yourself."

77. Reference to the Qur'an 33:72: "Verily, We offered the trust to the heavens and the earth and the mountains, but they refused to bear it and were afraid of it, but man undertook it..."

78. Reference to the Qur'an 3:33–34: "Verily, Allah chose Adam and Noah and the descendants of Abraham and the descendants of 'Imran above all creatures, offspring one of the other."

79. On Salman, see note 73 above.

80. 'Abd al-Salam Shah (d. c. 890/1493) and Mustansir bi'llah III, also known as Gharib Mirza (d. 904/1498), were the 33rd and 34th Ismaili Imams in whose time there was a significant revival of Ismaili intellectual and literary activity in Iran.

81. *Mawla*, meaning lord, master, guide, in the sense used by the Prophet at Ghadir Khumm: "'Ali is the *mawla* of those whose *mawla* I am."

82. Reference to the Qur'an 2:117: "(God is) the Originator of the heavens and the earth. When He decrees a thing, He says to it 'Be!' and it is."

83. On Khayrkhwah-i Harati's notion of the "three worlds", comprising the peoples of oneness (*wahda*), gradation (*tarattub*) and opposition (*tadadd*), see his *Fasl dar bayan-i shinakht-i imam*, ed. W. Ivanow (Tehran, 1960); Eng. tr. W. Ivanow, *On the Recognition of the Imam* (Bombay, 1947).

84. On Salman, see note 73 above.

85. Reference to the Qur'an 14: 24–25: "A goodly word like a goodly tree, whose root is firmly fixed and its branch is in the heaven – it brings

forth its fruit at all times, by the leave of its Lord."
86. Reference to the Qur'an 3:33–34. See note 78 above.
87. The poet evokes the Prophetic tradition: "I and 'Ali are from the same light."
88. An allusion to the Prophetic tradition: "The position of the people of my house (family) among you is like that of Noah's ark: he who boards it is saved, and he who stays behind is drowned."
89. By the trustworthy spirit (*al-ruh al-amin*), the poet means Gabriel, the angel of revelation, who is also identified with the Holy Spirit (*al-ruh al-quds*).
90. On the Pleiades, see note 55 above.
91. On the expression "proofs of His authority", see note 3 above.
92. Collyrium, a traditional, topical remedy for disorders of the eyes.
93. On *Haydar*, see note 24 above.
94. The battle of Khaybar in 7/628 was one of the decisive events in the mission of the Prophet Muhammad, during which Imam 'Ali played a crucial role in ensuring victory for the Muslims.
95. On Dhu'l-faqar, see note 17 above.
96. Reference to the Qur'an 3:103. See note 76 above.
97. Sultan Muhammad Shah, Aga Khan III (1877–1957), the 48th Ismaili Imam, was born in Karachi and succeeded to the Imamate in 1885. During his Imamate, the longest in Ismaili history, he initiated the modernization of the Ismaili community, establishing important communal institutions. He also participated actively on the international scene and advocated the rights of the Muslims.
98. Luqman, a figure of ancient Arabia who is cited in the Qur'an (31:12–19) as a monotheist sage. In later Arabic tradition, he is mentioned as the source of numerous fables and proverbs.
99. Abu'l-Hasan, the father of Hasan, i.e. Imam 'Ali.
100. The "five treasures of religion" are the Prophet Muhammad, Imam 'Ali, Fatima, Hasan and Husayn, also known in Shi'ism as *panj tan-i pak* (the pure pentad).
101. Reference to the Qur'an 15:29: "When I have fashioned him (Adam), and breathed into him My Spirit, fall ye down in obeisance to him."
102. Cornelian, a reddish-white precious or semi-precious stone.
103. Reference to the Qur'an 24:35–36: "Allah is the light of the heavens and the earth. The parable of His light is as if there were a niche and within it a lamp...."
104. His Highness Shah Karim al-Husayni, Aga Khan IV is the present 49th Imam of the Ismailis. He was born in 1936 in Geneva, educated at Le Rosey in Switzerland and Harvard University, and succeeded to the Imamate in 1957. Under his leadership, there has been a major transformation of the Ismaili community through the development of an extensive network of social, economic, educational and cultural institu-

tions, mainly in Africa, Asia, Europe and North America. He also heads the Aga Khan Foundation, which is one of the world's leading, non-governmental, development organizations.

Bibliography

al-Anashid al-diniyya. Salamiyya, Syria, 1973.

Asani, Ali. "The Ismaili *Ginans* as Devotional Literature", in *Devotional Literature in South Asia*, ed. R.S. McGregor. Cambridge, 1992, pp. 101–12.

———— "The Ginan Literature of the Ismailis of Indo-Pakistan: Its Origins, Characteristics and Themes", in *Devotion Divine: Bhakti Traditions from the Regions of India*, ed. Diana L. Eck and François Mallison. Gröningen–Paris, 1991, pp. 1–18.

Bausani, Alessandro. "Can We Speak of Muslim Poetry?", in *International Islamic Colloquium Papers*. Lahore, 1960, pp. 13–18.

Bellamy, James A. "The Impact of Islam on Early Arabic Poetry", in *Islam: Past Influence and Present Challenge*, ed. Alford T. Welch and Pierre Cachia. Edinburgh, 1979, pp. 141-67.

Browne, Edward G. *A Literary History of Persia.* Cambridge, 1902–1924.

Bruijn, J.T.P. de "The Religious Use of Persian Poetry", in *Studies on Islam*. Amsterdam, 1974, pp. 63–74.

The Cambridge History of Arabic Literature: Arabic Literature to the End of the Umayyad Period, ed. A.F.L. Beeston et al. Cambridge, 1983.

The Cambridge History of Arabic Literature: 'Abbasid Belles-Lettres, ed. Julia Ashtiany et al. Cambridge, 1990.

Corbin, Henry. *History of Islamic Philosophy*, tr. L. Sherrard. London, 1993.

———— and M.Mu'in, eds. *Commentaire de la qasida ismaélienne d'Abu'l-Haitham Jorjani*. Tehran–Paris, 1955.

Daftary, Farhad. *The Assassin Legends: Myths of the Isma'ilis*. London, 1994.

———— *The Isma'ilis: Their History and Doctrines*. Cambridge, 1990.

Dewhurst, R.P. "Abu Tammam and Ibn Hani", *Journal of the Royal Asiatic Society* (1926), pp. 629–42.

The Encyclopaedia of Islam, ed. H.A.R. Gibb et al. New ed. Leiden–London, 1960–.

Fida'i Khurasani, Muhammad b. Zayn al-'Abidin. *Mathnawi-i nigaristan*, ed. A.N. Semenov, in "Ismailitsky panegirik obozhestvlennoma 'Aliyu Fedai Khorasonskogo'", *Iran*, 3 (1929), pp. 51–70.

Gabrieli, Francesco. "Religious Poetry in Early Islam", in *Arabic Poetry: Theory and Development*, ed. G.E. von Grunebaum. Wiesbaden, 1973, pp. 5–17.

Grunebaum, G.E.von. "The Early Development of Islamic Religious Poetry", *Journal of the American Oriental Society*, 60 (1940), pp. 23–9.

Ibn Hani, Muhammad. *Tabiyin al-ma'ani fi sharh diwan ibn Hani al-Andalusi al-Maghribi*, ed. Zahid 'Ali. Cairo, 1933.

—— *The Diwan of Abu Qasim Muhammad ibn Hani al-Andalusi*, tr. A. Wormhoudt. Oskaloosa, Iowa, 1985.

Hasan-i Sabbah. *Munajat-i Baba Sayyidna*, in *Kitab al-manaqib*. Karachi, 1986.

Hodgson, Marshall G.S. *The Venture of Islam*. Chicago, 1974.

Hooda, V.N. "Some Specimens of Satpanth Literature", in *Collectanea*, vol. 1, ed. W. Ivanow. Leiden, 1948, pp. 55–137.

Hunzai, 'Allama Nasir al-Din. *Bihiste Asquring*. Karachi, 1988.

—— *Jawahir-i haqa'iq*. Karachi, 1975.

—— *Jawahir-i ma'arif*, Karachi, n.d.

Ivanow, W. *Ismaili Literature: A Bibliographical Survey*. Tehran, 1963.

—— "An Ismaili Poem in Praise of the Fidawis", *Journal of the Bombay Branch of the Royal Asiatic Society*, New Series, 14 (1938), pp. 63–72.

Jayyusi, Salma K. "Umayyad Poetry", in *The Cambridge History of Arabic Literature: Arabic Literature to the End of the Umayyad Period*, ed. A.F.L. Beeston et al. Cambridge, 1983, pp. 387–432.

Kashani, Abu'l-Qasim 'Abd Allah b. 'Ali. *Zubdat al-tawarikh: bakhsh-i Fatimiyan va Nizariyan*, ed., M.T. Danishpazhuh. 2nd ed., Tehran, 1987.

Khaki Khurasani, Imam Quli. *An Abbreviated Version of the Diwan of Khaki Khurasani*, ed. W. Ivanow. Bombay, 1933.

Khayrkhwah-i Harati, Muhammad Rida b. Sultan Husayn. *Tasnifat-i Khayrkhwah-i Harati*, ed. W. Ivanow. Tehran, 1961.

—— *Fasl dar bayan-i shinakht-i imam*, ed. W. Ivanow. Tehran, 1960; English trans.,W. Ivanow, *On the Recognition of the Imam*. 2nd ed., Bombay, 1947.

Kitab al-manaqib. Karachi, 1986.

Madelung, Wilferd. "The *Hashimiyyat* of al-Kumayt and Hashimi Shi'ism", *Studia Islamica*, 70 (1989), pp. 5–26; reprinted in his *Religions and Ethnic Movements in Medieval Islam*. London, 1992, article V.

Massignon, Louis. *The Passion of Mansur al-Hallaj: Mystic and Martyr of Islam*, tr. Herbert Mason. Princeton, 1982.

Meisami, Julie Scott. "Symbolic Structure in a Poem by Nasir-i-Khusrau", *Iran: Journal of the British Institute of Persian Studies*, 31 (1993), pp. 103–117.

al-Mu'ayyad fi'l-Din al-Shirazi, Abu Nasr Hibat Allah b. Abi 'Imran Musa. *Diwan*, ed. Muhammad K. Husayn. Cairo, 1949.

Nanji, Azim. *The Nizari Isma'ili Tradition in the Indo-Pakistan Subcontinent*. Delmar, NY, 1978.

Nasir-i Khusraw. *Diwan*, ed. N. Taqawi. Tehran, 1925–28; ed. M. Minuwi and M. Muhaqqiq. Tehran, 1974.

—— *Make a Shield from Wisdom: Selected Verses from Nasir-i Khusraw's Divan*, tr. Annemarie Schimmel. London, 1993.

Bibliography

———— *Nasir-i Khusraw: Forty Poems from the Divan*, tr. Peter Lamborn Wilson and Gholam Reza Aavani. Tehran, 1977.

Nasr, S. Hossein. "Shi'ism and Sufism: Their Relationship in Essence and in History", in his *Sufi Essays*. New York, 1977, pp. 104–20.

Nizari Quhistani, Hakim Sa'd al-Din. *Diwan*, ed. Muzahir Musaffa. Tehran, 1992.

al-Nu'man b. Muhammad, al-Qadi Abu Hanifa. *al-Urjuza al-mukhtara*, ed. Ismail K. Poonawala. Montreal, 1970.

Poonawala, Ismail K. *Biobibliography of Isma'ili Literature*. Malibu, Ca., 1977.

Rubinacci, R. "Political Poetry", in *The Cambridge History of Arabic Literature: 'Abbasid Belles-Lettres*, ed. Julia Ashtiany et al. Cambridge, 1990, pp. 185–201.

Rumi, Jalal al-Din. *Kulliyyat-i Shams Tabrizi*. Lucknow, 1930.

Schimmel, Annemarie. *And Muhammad is His Messenger: The Veneration of the Prophet in Islamic Piety*. Chapel Hill, NC, 1985.

———— *As Through a Veil: Mystical Poetry in Islam*. New York, 1982.

———— *Mystical Dimensions of Islam*. Chapel Hill, NC, 1975.

Shabistari, Mahmud. *Gulshan-i raz*, ed. and tr. E.H. Whinfield. London, 1880.

Shackle, Christopher and Zawahir Moir. *Ismaili Hymns from South Asia: An Introduction to the Ginans*. London, 1992.

Smoor, Pieter. "The Poet's House: Fiction and Reality in the Works of the 'Fatimid' Poets", *Quaderni di Studi Arabi*, 10 (1992), pp. 45–62.

———— "Wine, Love and Praise for the Fatimid Imams, the Enlightened of God", *Zeitschrift der Deutschen Morgenländischen Gesellschaft*, 142 (1992), pp. 90–104.

———— "Fatimid Poets and the 'Takhallus' that Bridges the Nights of Time to the Imam of Time", *Der Islam*, 68 (1991), pp. 232–62.

Stern, S.M. "Ja'far ibn Mansur al-Yaman's Poems on the Rebellion of Abu Yazid", in his *Studies in Early Isma'ilism*. Jerusalem–Leiden, 1983, pp. 146–52.

Tamim b. al-Mu'izz al-Fatimi. *Diwan*, ed. M.H. al-A'zami et al. Cairo, 1957.

Taylor, J.B. "Ja'far al-Sadiq, Spiritual Forbear of the Sufis", *Islamic Culture*, 40 (1966), pp. 97–113.

Index of First Lines

General Index